Uganda

Uganda

Revised Edition

BY ETTAGALE BLAUER
AND JASON LAURÉ

Enchantment of the World™
Second Series

Children's Press®

An Imprint of Scholastic Inc.

NEW YORK TORONTO LONDON AUCKLAND SYDNEY
MEXICO CITY NEW DELHI HONG KONG
DANBURY, CONNECTICUT

Frontispiece: Nkusi Falls on Lake Albert

Consultant: Nelson M. Kasfir, Professor of African and African American Studies, Dartmouth College, Hanover, New Hampshire

Please note: All statistics are as up-to-date as possible at the time of publication.

Book production by Herman Adler

Library of Congress Cataloging-in-Publication Data

Blauer, Ettagale.
  Uganda / by Ettagale Blauer and Jason Lauré. — 2nd series.
    p. cm. — (Enchantment of the world)
  Includes bibliographical references and index.
  ISBN-13: 978-0-531-20655-3
  ISBN-10: 0-531-20655-6
  1. Uganda—Juvenile literature. [1. Uganda.] I. Lauré, Jason II. Title. III. Series.
  DT433.222.B58 2009
  967.61—dc22   2008044189

© 2010 by Scholastic Inc.
All rights reserved. Published in 2010 by Children's Press, an imprint of Scholastic Inc.
Published simultaneously in Canada.
Printed in China

SCHOLASTIC, CHILDREN'S PRESS, and associated logos are trademarks and/or registered trademarks of Scholastic Inc.
1 2 3 4 5 6 7 8 9 10 R 19 18 17 16 15 14 13 12 11 10   62

Uganda

Contents

Cover photo:
Girl carrying bananas

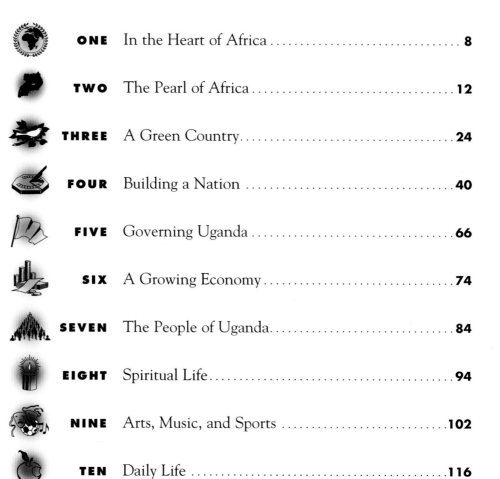

Western Uganda

Ugandan children

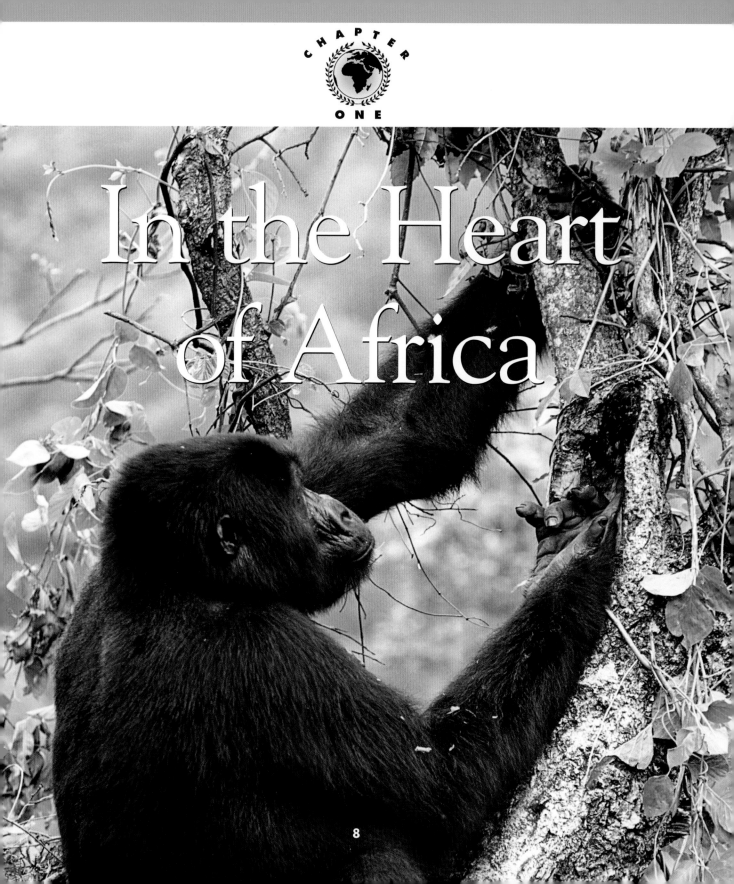

In the Heart of Africa

UGANDA LIES NESTLED IN THE HEART OF AFRICA. IT IS one of the most beautiful countries on the continent, boasting a rich and varied landscape ranging from towering mountains to a vast plateau. Uganda is one of the few places where visitors can get a close look at mountain gorillas, one of the animal kingdom's gentle giants. The gorillas live quietly in this lushly forested country, one of the greenest parts of Africa.

Though Uganda is landlocked, it is rich in rivers and lakes. Visitors enjoy white-water rafting, while Ugandans feast on the fish found there. The fertile farmland enables people to feed themselves through bad times as well as good.

Opposite: **A mountain gorilla makes a meal of termites in the forest tree-tops. Mountain gorillas live only in Uganda, Congo, and Rwanda.**

Ugandan fishers paddle on Lake Victoria, the largest lake in Africa.

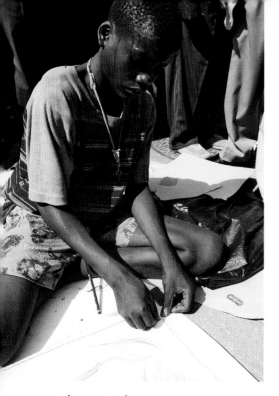

Sylvester Nsubuga earns money by drawing portraits of passersby in Kampala.

Uganda has had a tumultuous history, and the people have survived war, disease, and oppressive governments. Because of these problems, Uganda is home to many orphans. Twelve-year-old Sylvester Nsubuga lost both his parents and his grandmother to AIDS, a disease that has devastated the country since the 1980s. Sylvester is a talented artist, which enables him to support himself and his younger brothers. He draws portraits on the streets of Kampala, the capital city, capturing a likeness in just a few minutes. When he works, a crowd usually gathers, watching the portrait come alive. He charges 3,000 shillings, a little less than US$3, for each portrait. He hopes to go back to school to learn to read and write.

Since 1986, Yoweri Museveni has been Uganda's president. Many people credit him with bringing the country stability. Others suggest he has ruled too long. As the country has grown more stable, its economy has grown. The improving economy can be seen on the streets of Kampala where people dash around on motorcycles called *boda-bodas*. Not too long ago, people were more likely to ride bicycles. Now, they ride past a new series of murals in the center of town that depict historic moments in Uganda's struggle for independence and democracy.

Oil was recently discovered in western Uganda. This natural resource could give the country a big boost by bringing in needed foreign currency. Uganda now faces the challenge of investing its oil income to build the country.

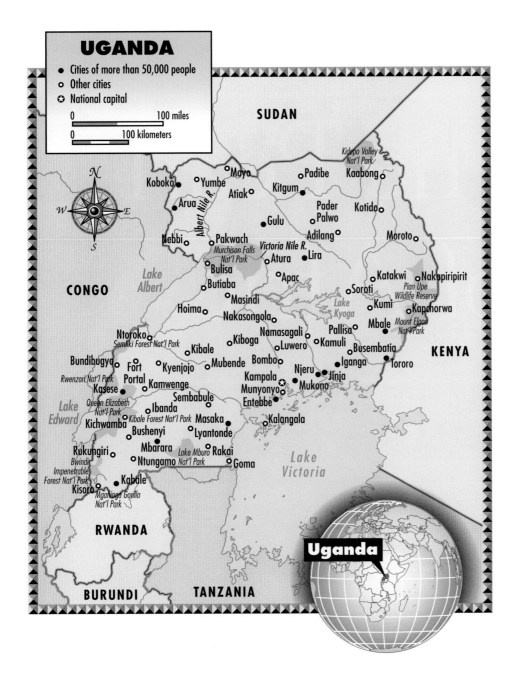

UGANDA

- Cities of more than 50,000 people
- Other cities
- National capital

0 ——————— 100 miles
0 ——————— 100 kilometers

SUDAN

Kidepo Valley Nat'l Park

Koboko
Yumbe
Moyo
Padibe
Kaabong
Arua
Atiak
Kitgum
Pader
Palwo
Kotido
Nebbi
Gulu
Adilang
Moroto
Pakwach
Victoria Nile R.
Murchison Falls Nat'l Park
Atura
Lira
Bulisa
Apac
Katakwi
Nakapiripirit
Butiaba
Soroti
Pian Upe Wildlife Reserve
Masindi
Lake Kyoga
Kumi
Kapchorwa
Hoima
Nakasongola
Pallisa
Mbale
Mount Elgon Nat'l Park
Ntoroko
Semliki Forest Nat'l Park
Kiboga
Namasagali
Kamuli
Kibale
Luwero
Busembatia
KENYA
Bundibugya
Kyenjojo
Mubende
Bombo
Iganga
Tororo
Fort Portal
Kamwenge
Njeru
Jinja
Rwenzori Nat'l Park
Kampala
Kasese
Munyonyo
Mukono
Queen Elizabeth Nat'l Park
Sembabule
Entebbe
Ibanda
Kichwamba
Kibale Forest Nat'l Park
Masaka
Kalangala
Lake Edward
Bushenyi
Lyantonde
Rukungiri
Mbarara
Lake Mburo Nat'l Park
Rakai
Lake Victoria
Ntungamo
Goma
Bwindi Impenetrable Forest Nat'l Park
Kabale
Kisoro
Mgahinga Gorilla Nat'l Park

Albert Nile R.

Lake Albert

CONGO

Lake Edward

RWANDA

BURUNDI

TANZANIA

Uganda

CHAPTER

TWO

The Pearl of Africa

12

The beautiful Sese Islands lie in the northwestern part of Lake Victoria.

U GANDA IS SO RICH IN NATURAL BEAUTY AND RESOURCES that former British prime minister Winston Churchill called it "the Pearl of Africa." Its total area of 91,134 square miles (236,037 square kilometers) makes it slightly smaller than the U.S. state of Oregon. Uganda lies in the center of Africa far from any ocean, but it is richly endowed with lakes and rivers. Lake Victoria, the largest lake on the continent, forms much of Uganda's southern border. The nations of Tanzania and Rwanda also border Uganda to the south. Lake Edward and Lake Albert make up part of Uganda's western border with Congo. Sudan forms the northern border, while Kenya lies due east.

Opposite: **Sipi Falls tumble over a cliff near Mount Elgon National Park, north of Mbale.**

Uganda's Geographic Features

Area: 91,134 square miles (236,037 sq km)

Highest Elevation: Margherita Peak on Mount Stanley, 16,763 feet (5,109 m)

Lowest Elevation: Lake Albert, 2,037 feet (621 m)

Longest River: Victoria Nile

Largest Lake: Victoria, the largest lake in Africa, 26,828 square miles (69,485 sq km)

Longest Border: 580 miles (933 km), with Kenya

Average High Temperatures: In Kampala, 82°F (28°C) in January, 77°F (25°C) in July

Average Low Temperatures: In Kampala, 64°F (18°C) in January, 63°F (17°C) in July

Driest Area: Gulu, 0.4 inches (1 cm) of rain in January

Wettest Area: Entebbe, 9.8 inches (25 cm) of rain in April

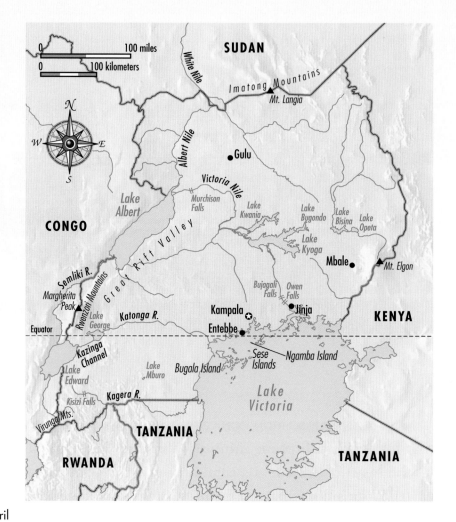

Plateau and Mountains

Much of Uganda is formed by a high plateau that lies about 3,000 feet (900 meters) above sea level. The land across this plateau is nearly flat. The plateau itself gradually slopes downward to the north. Its elevation declines from about 4,300 feet

(1,300 m) above sea level in the south to 2,460 feet (750 m) in the north.

Mountain chains nearly encircle the country's land borders. The Rwenzori Mountains run for about 50 miles (80 km) along the border with Congo. Even in ancient times, they were known as "the Mountains of the Moon," a nickname they may have been given because their snowcapped peaks looked white, like the moon. The highest point in Uganda is in the Rwenzoris. Margherita Peak on Mount Stanley rises 16,763 feet (5,109 m) high. This makes it the third-highest peak in all of Africa. Margherita Peak is usually covered in snow and ice and often shrouded in clouds.

Mount Baker is one of six major peaks that make up the rugged Rwenzori Mountains.

Just to the south of the Rwenzoris lie the volcanic Virunga Mountains. This chain separates Uganda from Rwanda and from the southwestern part of Congo. Across the border in Congo lies Mount Nyiragongo, one of the most active volcanoes in Africa. Uganda's border with Kenya is also marked by volcanic mountains. Mount Elgon, which stands 14,178 feet (4,321 m) high, is the tallest peak in this mountain chain. In the north, Uganda is separated from Sudan by the Imatong Mountains and Mount Langia, which stands 9,937 feet (3,029 m) high.

Lush vegetation blankets the foothills below Mount Elgon.

Bunyoni and many other lakes lie in southern Uganda. About 15 percent of Uganda's total area is covered by water.

Lakes and Rivers

Viewed on a map, the southern part of Uganda looks like a group of islands because so many lakes and rivers break up the land. In the 19th century, European explorers traveled these waters seeking to unravel one of the great mysteries of the time: the source of the mighty Nile River. The explorers named many of the waterways after themselves and other Europeans.

A man prepares his fishing boat on the shores of Lake Victoria. The lake is an important transportation route for people in Uganda, Tanzania, and Kenya.

Lake Victoria, also known as Ukerewe and Nalubaale, is one of the sources of the Nile River. It is the most important lake in Uganda—and in all of Africa—and the second-widest freshwater lake in the world. Only Lake Superior, one of the Great Lakes in North America, has a larger surface area. Large boats carry passengers and freight from Uganda across the immense lake to ports in Kenya and Tanzania. The lake contains 84 islands called the Sese Islands. Some of the larger islands are inhabited. The largest, Bugala Island, is a popular site for hiking, camping, and fishing.

Looking at Uganda's Cities

Uganda's largest city by far is its capital, Kampala. According to the 2002 census, it is home to about 1.2 million people.

Gulu is Uganda's second-largest city, with a population of about 119,000. It is the economic center of northern Uganda. Much of northern Uganda's agricultural output is processed and shipped in the city.

The city of Jinja, in southeastern Uganda, began as a fishing village. Today, it is an important port and Uganda's third-largest city, with a population of about 86,000. The former Ripon Falls in Jinja is considered to be the source of the White Nile River. Today, that

waterfall is submerged under the waters behind Nalubaale Dam (above). Electricity generated by the dam's hydroelectric plant serves most of Uganda. Jinja is the most popular tourist site in Uganda. Many people come to the region to enjoy white-water rafting.

Mbale (left), the fourth-largest city with a population of about 70,000, lies at the base of Mount Elgon 120 miles (190 km) northeast of Kampala. It is in the heart of a coffee-growing region and serves as an important trade center for agricultural products. The city is also the site of the Islamic University of Mbale.

Lake Victoria

In 1858, John Hanning Speke, a British explorer, was the first European to see the huge body of water now called Lake Victoria. He and another explorer, named Richard Burton, began their expedition together but then split up to search separately for the source of the Nile. Burton was furious when he found out that Speke had claimed this achievement for himself. In 1862, Speke named the lake after Queen Victoria of Great Britain, who would rule from 1837 to 1901. She is the longest-ruling monarch in British history. During Victoria's rule, the size of the British Empire doubled to include New Zealand, India, Egypt, and South Africa.

Lake Edward (also known as Lake Rutanzige) and Lake Albert (also called Albert Nyanza) are found in the western part of Uganda. Lake Edward is linked to the smaller Lake George (also called Lake Dweru) by a waterway called the Kazinga Channel. These three lakes lie in the western part of the Great Rift Valley, a huge trough in eastern Africa that stretches for thousands of miles from Ethiopia to Mozambique.

Ugandan men use weighted nets to catch fish in Lake Albert.

Another major lake, Kyoga, lies in the center of the country. It has "fingers" that fan out to form smaller seasonal lakes, including Kwania and Bugondo. Nearby lie two shallow lakes, Bisina and Opeta. During the dry season, Lake Opeta shrinks until it separates from Kyoga, the "mother" lake. When seasonal rains come and the water levels rise, the two lakes merge into one again.

Uganda has eight major rivers and many smaller ones. The most important is the Nile River, the longest river in Africa. In Uganda, it is known as the Victoria Nile. The river runs northward out of Lake Victoria, widening until it empties into Lake Kyoga. The Victoria Nile continues on to Lake Albert, and when it emerges there, it is known as the Albert Nile. The river then continues north until it crosses into Sudan, where it is known as the White Nile, and eventually merges with another river called the Blue Nile. The Nile is a lifeline for many of the people who live along its shores.

The Nile is the world's longest river. It runs the length of Uganda during its 4,135-mile (6,655 km) journey from central Africa north to the Mediterranean Sea.

Other main rivers include the Kazinga Channel and the Katonga and the Semliki rivers. Some rivers that are navigable in wet seasons may be impassable at other times, becoming nothing but swampy land. Many other rivers that are marked on maps may disappear entirely during dry seasons.

In the mountains where Uganda's rivers begin their journeys, their water is clear. As the rivers flow downstream, they pick up silt and the water becomes clouded.

Climate

Temperatures in Uganda are generally mild to warm throughout the year. In the northern part of the country, near Sudan, temperatures exceed 86 degrees Fahrenheit (30 degrees Celsius) most of the year. Much of the rest of the country enjoys a moderate climate, with temperatures ranging from 60°F to 80°F (16°C to 27°C), depending on the elevation.

Most of Uganda receives adequate amounts of rain, but the rain falls in distinct seasons. The dry northeastern part of the country gets about 20 inches (50 centimeters) of rain per year. The north has an erratic wet season that usually starts in April and lasts until October. Rain can fall anytime during that period and is unpredictable. The wettest region

The Middle of the World

The equator is an imaginary line that runs around the middle of the earth, halfway between the North Pole and the South Pole. It divides the Northern Hemisphere from the Southern Hemisphere. The equator runs through Uganda; about three-quarters of the country lying north of the equator and one-quarter lying south of it. Because Uganda lies on the equator, days and nights are of equal length throughout the year.

is around the Sese Islands in Lake Victoria, where 80 inches (200 cm) of rain falls, mostly during the wet seasons. In the south, the wet seasons occur in April and May, and then again in October and November. The "dry" months in between are often marked by tropical thunderstorms.

Heavy rainfalls sometimes cause major flooding in Uganda. In November 2007, floodwaters rose in Kampala.

A Green Country

UGANDA HAS ONE OF THE RICHEST NATURAL ENVIRONMENTS in Africa. It has immense natural parks and wildlife reserves and vast forests of lush greenery. These forests provide habitat to a wide variety of animals, including gorillas, chimpanzees, elephants, rhinoceroses, antelope, and hundreds of bird species.

Opposite: **Giraffes are the tallest living land animals in the world.**

Pelicans are common near Uganda's lakes and rivers.

Tracking Gorillas

Mountain gorillas are the largest primates in the world. Males generally weigh from 300 to 400 pounds (140 to 180 kilograms). Bwindi Impenetrable Forest National Park and Mgahinga Gorilla National Park were established to protect these highly endangered creatures. Both parks are in the southwest corner of Uganda, bordering Congo and Rwanda. Each day, a small number of visitors are permitted into Bwindi in the company of a skilled tracker to look for the gorillas, which are constantly on the move. Though experienced guides keep track of the gorilla families' movements, it can still take up to five hours of difficult hiking to find them. Once a gorilla family is located, the visitors must sit quietly to observe the gorillas as they go about their daily life. Gorillas spend much of their time eating the vegetation that surrounds them. They have a very close and nurturing family life.

Only about 700 mountain gorillas survive today, roughly 340 of them in Bwindi Impenetrable Forest National Park. Though this number is small, it is a great success story. The gorillas' numbers have increased from fewer than 600 in the mid-1990s.

Chimpanzees can survive in many habitats, but they prefer wooded areas. They eat fruits, nuts, seeds, leaves, flowers, insects, and some small mammals.

Apes and Monkeys

The great apes are a family of mammals also known as primates. Two of the four ape species are found in Uganda, the gorilla and the chimpanzee. Gorillas are the largest of the group, with adult males growing to a height of 6 feet (1.8 m). They are vegetarians and spend their days munching their way through the forests.

The common chimpanzee lives in large communities of one dominant male and other related males. Female chimpanzees move among communities with their young. Remarkably, mothers and their sons may remain in close relationships in the wild for more than 40 years. Daughters, on the other hand, usually leave their mothers when they are mature and ready to start their own families. Groups of chimpanzees live in specific territories and defend their territory against

outsiders. Chimpanzees are primarily fruit eaters, but they also hunt smaller mammals, especially monkeys. Chimpanzees are extremely intelligent animals that use tools such as stones to help them open nuts.

The chimpanzee population in Uganda is highly threatened. People sometimes kill them for food. They are also losing their habitat as farms and cities expand. Some people capture chimpanzees and sell them as pets, but the creatures remain wild and a threat to people. Ngamba Island Chimpanzee Sanctuary rescues pet chimps that were abandoned by owners after they grew too large. It also rescues babies that were orphaned when their parents were killed.

Many other species of mammals live in Uganda, including at least ten species of monkeys. The blue monkey is found in most of the country's forests. Red-tailed monkeys are found in many areas, and the red colobus monkey, which lives in groups of 50 animals, is found mainly in Kibale Forest National Park, in the southwest.

Carnivores are meat-eating animals. Uganda is home to 38 species of carnivore mammals. The largest are lions. In Uganda, lions make their homes mainly around Murchison Falls National Park, in the northwest, and Queen Elizabeth National Park, in the southwest. Lions usually live in groups; these groups are called prides.

Uganda is also home to the leopard, a solitary animal with a spotted coat. Leopards like to climb trees, where they are difficult to see. Although leopards live throughout Uganda's national parks and forest reserves, they are most often seen on the Channel Track in Queen Elizabeth National Park.

Lions are skilled hunters. They will eat almost any animal they can chase down.

Cheetahs, which also sport a spotted coat, are the fastest land mammals, able to run 70 miles per hour (113 kph) over a short distance. They use their great speed to chase down prey. Because they eat only fresh meat, they must hunt much more often than lions. Lions may feast on a kill for a longer time. Cheetahs are found only around Kidepo Valley National Park, in the northeast.

Smaller cats found in Uganda include the caracal and the African golden cat. Other carnivores in Uganda include the spotted hyena, the African civet, the genet, the honey badger, and the mongoose.

Unlike most cats, cheetahs cannot climb trees. They make up for this with their incredible speed, sometimes reaching speeds of 70 mph (113 kph).

Herbivores

Herbivores are animals that eat only plants. The largest land animal in the world, the African elephant, is a herbivore. Male African elephants stand about 12 feet (3.5 m) high and weigh 12,000 pounds (5,500 kg). Females are generally smaller, standing about 10 feet (3 m) high. Female elephants form strong family groups. Male elephants leave their group when they reach maturity, at around age 12; females remain close and may live together for up to 50 years. Elephants live in almost all of Uganda's national parks.

Adult elephants consume 300 to 400 pounds (135 to 180 kg) of food per day. They eat grass, leaves, twigs, bark, fruit, and other plant parts.

The Rise and Fall—and Rise Again—of a Park

Murchison Falls National Park is the largest preserve in Uganda. It is named for one of its main attractions, Murchison Falls, a narrow but extremely powerful outlet for the Victoria Nile. At this point in its journey, the river must squeeze through a tiny gap. When it emerges, it shoots out over a cliff in a spectacular display.

Murchison Falls National Park spreads west from the northwestern shore of Lake Albert. The vast area it covers was once infested with tsetse flies, which carry African trypanosomiasis, also known as sleeping sickness. This disease can cause convulsions and often death. The tsetse flies made the region unsuitable for human habitation. But by 1954, the flies were eliminated and the area was turned into a national park. In 1972, the park was closed when Uganda's dictatorial ruler, Idi Amin, banned all foreign visitors to the country.

In the 1960s, an estimated 14,500 elephants lived in the park. But not long after the park was closed, illegal hunters, known as poachers, began targeting the elephants and other wildlife. Then the military began hunting the animals for food. By 1990, the park's wildlife was nearly gone. All that remained were about 250 elephants and small herds of antelope and buffalo.

In the years since, peace has returned to Uganda, and the wildlife has started to recover. The elephant population is now estimated at more than 1,100, and the buffalo population has reached more than 8,000. Giraffes, lions, and antelope such as kobs, bushbucks, waterbucks, and hartebeests have also returned. The park is also home to colobus monkeys, chimpanzees, and an astounding variety of birds. More than 460 bird species have been spotted there.

Twenty-nine species of antelope live in Uganda, including the eland, the largest antelope in the world. This huge beast, which stands 6 feet (1.8 m) tall, looks somewhat like a cow with dramatic twisted horns. The kudu is a beautiful antelope with a gray-brown coat. Adult males have great spiraling horns. Other antelope found in Uganda are hartebeests, roan antelope, topi, and little Grant's gazelles. Only about 100 of these gazelles still live in Uganda.

The topi are among the many antelope species that live in Uganda. Both male and female topi have thick, ringed horns.

Other herbivores in Uganda include rhinoceroses, African buffalo, giraffes, Burchell's zebra, and hippopotamuses. Although hippopotamuses look slow and sleepy, they can actually move quickly and are very aggressive. They kill more people than any other mammal in Africa. Hippopotamuses can be found in most of Uganda's lakes and are common in Murchison Falls, Queen Elizabeth, and Lake Mburo national parks.

Hippopotamuses spend the daylight hours in the water. At night, they move onto land to graze.

The National Bird

The gray-crowned crane, also called the crested crane, is Uganda's national bird. It is featured on the national flag. Some people say that it was chosen as the national bird because its feathers contain all the colors of the flag. The distinctive golden feathers on its head, which stick straight up, make it easy to spot. The body is mainly gray, but the head features red skin and white patches, with a distinctive red sack under the chin. The bird stands 3 feet (1 m) tall and prefers swampy areas and grasslands.

Birdlife

Uganda has a remarkable number and diversity of birds. More than 1,000 species have been seen there. Uganda boasts 7 species of hornbills, 5 species of honeyguides, 7 species of woodpeckers, 13 species of thrushes, 8 species of sunbirds, 8 species of weavers, and 3 species of kingfishers. It is also home to ostriches, pelicans, Goliath herons, Marabou storks, African fish eagles, and Bateleur eagles. The African jacana, a bird that appears to walk on water as it walks across floating lily pads, also lives in Uganda.

The shoebill is a rare bird that lives primarily in swamplands.

Nature in the City

The countryside is full of wildlife, but some city residents don't have to go very far to see wild animals. The Uganda Wildlife Education Centre is located in the town of Entebbe, on Lake Victoria. The wildlife found there includes rhinoceroses, chimpanzees, Nile crocodiles, lions, monkeys, and birds.

The Entebbe Botanical Gardens were laid out in 1898 and have an extensive collection of native plants. More than 300 species can be seen here, including 200 that are native to Uganda. The garden introduces visitors to 120 plants with known medicinal value. It also shows species from many other lands.

Water Life

Uganda's lakes are home to many species of fish including the Nile perch, crayfish, and tiger fish. Nile perch can be enormous, often weighing as much as 440 pounds (200 kg). The lakes are also home to other large creatures, such as the Nile crocodile, the largest living reptile. Nile crocodiles can grow to be 20 feet (6 m) long. Although fishers fear the crocodiles, the reptiles prefer to eat fish. They will, however, kill an unfortunate lion or wildebeest that drinks from the lake.

The Nile crocodile has from 64 to 68 teeth. Its powerful jaw makes it a fearsome predator.

Plant Life

The diverse animal life of Uganda depends on the rich plant life found there. Uganda's great diversity of plant life is a result of its many different habitats, from snowcapped mountains to lush forests to near-desert conditions. Bamboo and plants in the senecio family grow on the upper reaches of mountain slopes. Mvule trees and elephant grass grow on the central plateau, while isolated acacia trees grow in the country's dry northern reaches. Swamp grass and papyrus crowd swampy

Senecio forests flourish high in the Rwenzori Mountains, near the edges of glaciers.

Solving the Hyacinth Problem

Although most plants help sustain animal and human life, one plant proved to be a killer in Uganda: the water hyacinth. It was introduced into the region because of its beautiful flowers, but it quickly spread out of control, causing the destruction of other plants and fish. Water hyacinths grew so thick in Lake Victoria that they closed some ports and nearly stopped boat traffic. This brought business to a halt because transportation across the lake is crucial to an area with few roads.

To solve the problem of the water hyacinths, Ugandans introduced two species of weevils into the lake. These beetles eat their way through the plants, feeding on the leaves. The weevils also lay eggs in the leaf stalks and the crowns of the water hyacinths, which stops the plants from growing and reproducing. This

program has been successfully combined with use of a machine that travels the waters of Lake Victoria, chopping up the great masses of water-hyacinth growth. Together, the weevils and the machine have helped bring the problem under control.

regions around lakes. The well-named Bwindi Impenetrable Forest is thick with ferns, vines, bamboo, orchids, and shrubs. The nation's forests are also filled with flowers such as blue clematis, red passion flower, and gloriosa lily, a climbing plant with scarlet and gold flowers that sometimes reaches heights of 15 feet (4.6 m).

In rural areas, people depend on wild plants for food. These plants enabled the people of Uganda to survive war-torn years when the nation's economy ground to a halt. Favorite fruits include wild plums and gooseberries. Pumpkins are important, too, not only for their flesh but also for their seeds, which can be cooked and eaten.

Building a Nation

TWO THOUSAND YEARS AGO, THE land now called Uganda was inhabited by people who were hunter-gatherers. Often called the "first people," they were forced out by other, more aggressive peoples who migrated from other parts of Africa in about 1000 CE. The newly arrived people became known as Bantu, a word that means "people." Some Bantu were farmers who grew crops in the fertile soil. Others grazed livestock on the grasslands. Though Bantu farmers thrived in the region, thanks to its good climate and growing conditions, their intense cultivation of the land over a period of several centuries gradually destroyed the dense forests that once covered the region around Lake Victoria.

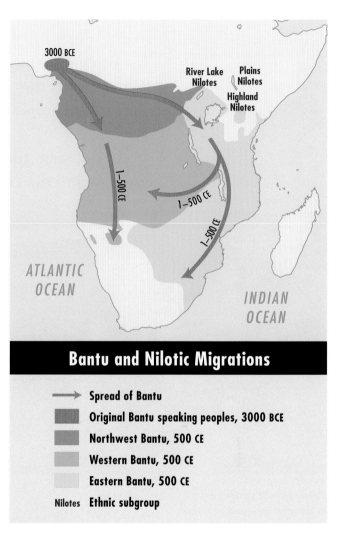

Bantu and Nilotic Migrations

→ Spread of Bantu
     Original Bantu speaking peoples, 3000 BCE
     Northwest Bantu, 500 CE
     Western Bantu, 500 CE
     Eastern Bantu, 500 CE
Nilotes Ethnic subgroup

As Bantu continued to arrive in great migrations, other newcomers also arrived. Nilotic people came in from the northeast, bringing a very different culture from that of the Bantu. These two groups, the Nilotic and the Bantu, made up most of Uganda's population.

Opposite: **This illustration of a Bantu chief dates to 1878.**

Farmers and Herders

The Bantu introduced bananas into the Uganda area in about 1000 CE, when they first arrived in the region. This nutritious fruit enabled people to settle around lakes, where the bananas grew well.

At the same time, the Nilotic people, who were herders, moved to the Lake Victoria area. Their cattle and other livestock needed to graze. As they used up the grasses in one area, they moved to another. The Nilotic people didn't settle in any particular region. Instead, they moved about. Their way of life is called seminomadic.

The Bantu and Nilotic peoples brought different skills to the region and had different ways of organizing and governing themselves. Eventually, kingdoms emerged. The two largest kingdoms in Uganda were Bunyoro and Buganda.

The Baganda people lived in what is now southeastern and eastern Uganda.

The Banyoro, as the people of Bunyoro are called, dominated the region northwest of Lake Victoria for several centuries. Like other kingdoms, Bunyoro was prone to civil wars and over who would rise to become king. These internal battles weakened the Banyoro's ability to maintain control over their territory.

The Baganda, the people of Buganda, settled on the north-western shore of Lake Victoria. This land was swampy and unsuitable for cattle grazing. The Baganda were the most successful of the four kingdoms in expanding their territory. The Buganda Kingdom was divided into counties, which were usually acquired by military conquest, particularly over the neighboring Bunyoro Kingdom. Buganda histories detail how the kingdom acquired each of 18 counties. The Baganda built roads and bridges to allow the kingdom's armies and tax collectors to travel to all parts of the kingdom.

The Baganda were organized into clans, large groups of people who were related to one another through one common ancestor. Each clan had its own chief. All the Baganda, including the chiefs, were ruled by one supreme leader, the *kabaka*.

In later years, after Europeans gained control of the region, the Ankole and Toro kingdoms also emerged. The Ankole Kingdom was located east of Lake Albert. Two major groups lived in the kingdom. The Bahima were cattle herders, and the Bairu were farmers. The Bahima dominated the kingdom. Toro, Uganda's fourth kingdom, lay west of Lake Victoria.

Four Kingdoms, 1894

- Ankole
- Buganda
- Bunyoro
- Toro
- —— Present-day Uganda

Traders Arrive

Uganda sits in the heart of Africa and was difficult for outsiders to reach. But by 1844, traders had begun to make their way to Buganda. Ahmed bin Ibrahim may have been the first Arab trader to reach the area. Arab traders, who had long been working along the east coast of Africa, wanted to acquire ivory, the material of elephant tusks. Ivory was used to make art, jewelry, furniture parts, and piano keys. The Arabs also traded guns, gunpowder, and cloth for people who had been forced into slavery. They traded the people as if they were just another product. The people were sold to plantation owners in the Caribbean and Brazil to plant and harvest their crops.

Suna, the kabaka of Buganda in the mid-1800s, allowed Ibrahim to trade in his area. Many Banyoro were sold as slaves to Ibrahim and other traders. Soon, a lively trade grew as caravans of traders followed Ibrahim to the region. The Banyoro, who were trying to compete with the Baganda, also worked with Arab traders, seeking to acquire guns to protect themselves.

Foreigners also entered other areas of Uganda, seeking its riches. In the far north of the country, slave raiders from Egypt and Sudan and hunters preying on elephants for their ivory forced the Acholi people to make deals.

The Search for the Nile

In the mid-19th century, Europeans had no knowledge of most of the civilizations that existed in the middle of Africa. Reaching central Africa required facing dangers and difficul-

ties such as insects that transmit deadly diseases, extreme heat, lack of water, no roads, and no accurate maps.

To British explorers, finding the source of the Nile River was an exciting challenge. Expeditions usually began on the island of Zanzibar, about 25 miles (40 km) off the east coast of Africa. On Zanzibar, explorers could buy supplies from Arab traders and hire Africans to carry equipment they needed for their journey. Once they were outfitted with supplies and equipment, they took a boat to the African mainland to begin their trek into the interior.

It was a dangerous journey into the unknown. British explorers John Hanning Speke and Richard Burton traveled to the shore of Lake Tanganyika in central Africa in 1857,

In the 1800s, Zanzibar was a center of trade and the starting point for many European expeditions into Africa. Here, traders to Zanzibar acquire the ivory tusks of elephants.

John Hanning Speke and James Grant discuss the discovery of the Nile with Samuel and Florence Baker, a British couple who explored Africa.

but they failed to find the source of the Nile. The next year, Speke set out again, this time heading for another great central African lake he had heard rumors of. With him were a British army officer named James Grant and hundreds of African men who carried their goods and cooked their food.

When Speke reached the territory of Kabaka Mutesa I, the leader of the Buganda Kingdom, he sent word ahead, asking for permission to enter. After two months of waiting, permission was granted. Speke brought many gifts for the kabaka, including a rifle. Talking through interpreters, Speke learned about the customs and way of life of the Baganda. Speke heard the people talk about the great river that flowed northward out of Lake Victoria. As soon as possible, he traveled to the point where the river emerged from the lake as a waterfall. At last, in July 1862, the mystery of the source of the Nile was revealed to the Western world. Speke named this waterfall Ripon Falls to honor a British politician, George Robinson, the 1st Marquess of Ripon.

Traders and explorers were not the only people who found the region attractive. Missionaries, who tried to convince others to convert to their religions, were making their way to the African interior at about the same time. Protestant missionaries from the Church Missionary Society of London arrived in Buganda in 1877. French Catholic missionaries followed two years later. Meanwhile, Arab traders were trying to convert the Baganda to Islam, their religion.

Missionaries built many churches in Uganda. This one is in Kilembe.

These conflicting demands put pressure on the Baganda. Kabaka Mwanga, their leader, tried to end the influence the new religions were having. As a result, Baganda who were Christian converts forcibly removed the kabaka from his position. After a four-year civil war, Protestant and Roman Catholic Baganda divided the Buganda Kingdom and chose a new kabaka who would carry out their wishes.

The battle for the souls of the Baganda was just the beginning of foreign influence in Uganda. Soon, the entire territory was the scene of intense competition among Germans, French, and British, all of whom wanted to control the region. The European nations believed that having colonies in Africa would make them more powerful. They also wanted Africa's rich mineral resources and land for plantations. At the Berlin Conference of 1884–1885, representatives of European powers drew lines on a map of Africa, dividing the continent among themselves. Few Europeans actually lived in these lands. In some instances, no European had even reached areas that were being claimed. At the time, the Europeans did not back up their claims to African land with military might or administrative control. But by 1914, most of Africa would be under European rule.

At the Berlin Conference, Germany and Great Britain agreed to divide East Africa. Germany took the part known as Tanganyika (now Tanzania), while Britain acquired the regions now known as Kenya and Uganda. But neither European power wanted to spend money or send government officials to take charge. Instead, they used trading companies that were already doing business in Africa. The British sent Captain Frederick Lugard of the Imperial British East Africa Company to administer the region for their government. In 1890, Lugard placed all of Buganda under the company's "protection."

The British soon expanded their claims in Uganda. They used their superior weapons, as well as the help of the Baganda chiefs, to fight a battle for Bunyoro. They first occupied Bunyoro, and then Acholiland and the rest of the northern region. In 1894, Britain declared a protectorate over Buganda, beginning the period of colonial rule in Uganda.

The territory the British "protected" soon expanded into the other kingdoms. In 1896, the protectorate took in the territories of Bunyoro, Toro, and Ankole. In the late 1890s, the British moved into the region of the Basoga, which lay between Lake Victoria and Lake Kyoga, and began making treaties with chiefs north of the Nile River. With these treaties, they were putting together the country now known as Uganda. When Kabaka Mwanga II of Buganda revolted against British rule in 1897, he was overthrown. His infant son was named the new kabaka.

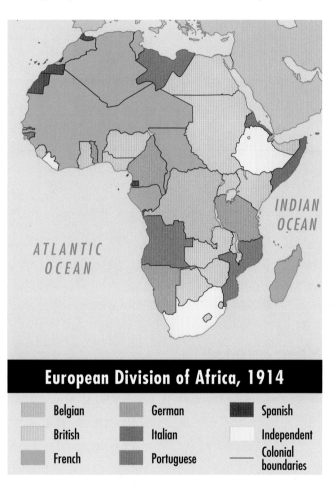

European Division of Africa, 1914

Belgian German Spanish

British Italian Independent

French Portuguese Colonial boundaries

Sir Harry Johnston was the British administrator in Uganda from 1899 to 1901. He worked out the Buganda Agreement.

Baganda Christians proved to be Britain's best allies. Their military support during the British fight for control was crucial. In 1900, the British sent Sir Harry Johnston to Uganda to govern the protectorate and to find a way to impose taxes on the local people. Taxes would provide funds for the British to enforce their rule. Johnston worked with the Baganda leaders to control the area.

The Buganda Agreement of 1900 granted Buganda self-governing status. The agreement recognized the kabaka as the ruler of Buganda, although still under British authority. The agreement also recognized his council of chiefs, called the Lukiiko. The chiefs were granted land in return for accepting the conditions of the agreement. To reward their supporters, the British gave the Baganda half the territory taken from the Banyoro. The Buganda Agreement remained in effect for more than 50 years.

Johnston also made agreements with the rulers of Toro, in 1900, and Ankole, in 1901. The Banyoro finally made a similar agreement with the British in 1933. The British were more involved in administering the regions north and east of the Nile because those areas did not have the four kingdoms' strong leaders and established political structures.

When the Baganda became the local tax collectors for the British, they imposed their language, customs, foods, and dress on the people they now administered, including the Banyoro. The Banyoro resented this and rose up against the Baganda in 1908. After this uprising, the British were forced to diminish the Baganda's role.

British East Africa

The British effort in Uganda was part of a much larger scheme to control all of East Africa and benefit from its resources. Because Uganda was far from the Indian Ocean ports where crops and goods could be shipped, the British allowed the region to be developed by Africans. Many British people found life in the tropics devastating to their health.

Lord Salisbury, the prime minister of Great Britain, supported the construction of a railroad in Uganda.

The Ugandans learned to farm on a commercial scale, growing cotton, the crop most highly desired by the British. Cotton brought cash to the Ugandans and helped supply textile mills in England.

The British prime minister, Lord Salisbury, strongly favored development of the region. Great Britain provided money to construct a railroad that would make Uganda easier to reach, enabling British settlers to transport their crops out of Africa.

Building a railroad in East Africa was a major step in transforming the region. The railroad started at the coast, in Kenya, and was later extended to Uganda. To build the railroad, the British turned to laborers from India, another British colony. These laborers, who were called "Asians" in Africa, would change the region forever. More than 30,000 men came to East Africa as indentured laborers, having signed a contract agreeing to work for a certain period of time. The indentured laborers were forced to work under the harshest conditions for

The construction of the Uganda Railway made it easier for farmers to transport their products out of Uganda.

A group of King's African Rifles moves along a flooded road in East Africa during World War I.

little pay. They often found that they had to pay their employers more for their food and housing than they earned. When their contracts were over, many returned to India. Meanwhile, other Indians moved to East Africa. They were not allowed to own land, so many opened small shops.

World War I began in 1914, as Great Britain and France fought Germany and Austria-Hungary. Uganda had a well-trained military that was part of the East African force known as the King's African Rifles. During World War I, this force grew to 16,000 members. The European war also spilled over into Africa itself. Many battles were fought between the British and the Germans in neighboring Tanganyika, which was a German colony. When Germany lost World War I, Tanganyika was put under the control of Great Britain.

A village in northern Uganda during the 1920s

Prosperity

Uganda's rich soil made it possible for the colony to support itself. The chief crop, cotton, was grown on land held by the Baganda chiefs. In Kenya, the British colonial government wanted British settlers to immigrate. In Uganda, however, the colonial government encouraged Ugandan farmers at the expense of British settlers.

The colonial administration in Uganda did not permit Africans to run businesses, so many Asians began running them. In time, Asians came to control some 80 percent of the economy.

In the 1920s, the rail line was extended to Soroti, at the northeastern tip of Lake Kyoga. Finally, Uganda had a way to transport its crops to ports on the Indian Ocean. Another rail line connected Kampala, the main city, with Mombasa on the Kenyan coast. These rail links gave rise to the idea among the British of uniting Uganda with Kenya and Tanganyika into a single "community." To the British, it was a way to reduce the cost of administering the three parts of the territory.

Africans, however, had been resisting the idea for years. Ugandans feared that white settlers in Kenya would dominate the territory. Many Europeans had immigrated to Kenya after World War I to escape the devastation the war had caused, and they now played a large role in the region. Black Africans and Asians worried about the British influence in Kenya.

Cotton continued to play a large role in Uganda's prosperity. With the income from cotton, many Baganda had enough money to plan for the future rather than just worry about their day-to-day existence. They bought bicycles and imported clothing. They also invested in education. Mainly thanks to Christian missions, literacy was already widespread in Uganda. Makerere University began as a technical school in Kampala in 1922. It was East Africa's first institution of higher education.

The Great Depression, a devastating worldwide economic downturn, struck in the 1930s, but Uganda managed well. Even when farmers could no longer sell their crops, they could still grow their own food.

The impact of World War II, which began in 1939, was felt directly in Uganda. The colonial government recruited more than 75,000 Ugandans to serve in the war. At the war's end, Ugandan troops remained in the military. They became a kind of domestic force, helping put down rebellions in neighboring Kenya. These troops became part of a force that was also used to suppress uprisings in their own country.

Baganda Demands

The British had been making economic decisions for the Baganda, and the Baganda wanted to manage their own affairs. They particularly wanted control over the sale of their crops on the open market. They also wanted to establish their own industry to process their cotton, which would increase their profits. The Baganda demanded political changes. They wanted to choose their own representatives in local government instead of having representatives appointed by the British. Resentment toward British policies grew and became violent. In 1949, some Baganda rioted.

In 1952, Sir Andrew Cohen took over Uganda as governor. He encouraged Ugandans to process their own cotton. He also changed the Legislative Council, a lawmaking body that the British had established. It would now consist

Sir Andrew Cohen (left) meets with Kabaka Mutesa II (on throne).

of Africans representing districts throughout Uganda. In this way, Cohen set up a political system that could serve the colony when it became an independent country.

Uganda was moving ahead in other fields as well. Its economy, based on cotton and coffee, was growing at a steady pace. This money was used in part to fund a hydroelectric dam on the Nile River in 1954.

In 1953, the question of joining Tanganyika and Kenya in a federation was raised once again. The Ugandans strongly opposed this plan. Kabaka Mutesa II refused to cooperate with the plans.

In response, Cohen had the kabaka deported to England. This was a devastating attack on the ruler, the very symbol of the Baganda, and it infuriated the peo-

Ugandans hold a parade celebrating Kabaka Mutesa II's return from England.

ple. After two years of Baganda opposition, Cohen was forced to allow the kabaka to return. When he came back, he was more powerful than before. For the first time since 1889, the kabaka could appoint or dismiss chiefs. He played a prominent role in governing Uganda.

Ugandans take part in an independence celebration in 1962.

Political Parties Form

Political parties, which had not been permitted before this time, began to spring up in Uganda. In 1952, Ignatius Musazi founded the Uganda National Congress (UNC). It was the first political organization that embraced many different cultures and had national aspirations. Some people considered the UNC too conservative. In 1960, they broke away to form the Uganda People's Congress (UPC). At this time, Britain announced that elections would soon be held. The UPC's leader was Milton Obote, a member of the Langi people, who live in north-central Uganda. A small ethnic group, the Langi often resented the Baganda, who controlled Ugandan politics.

Some Roman Catholics also felt left out of the decision-making process because the kabaka was always a Protestant. Many of them joined the new Democratic Party.

Another political party, Kabaka Yekka (KY), which means "King Alone," formed in June 1961. Obote made an agreement with the KY that the kabaka would be Uganda's ceremonial head of state.

In 1962, elections were held, and the UPC and the KY won most of the seats in Parliament. Together, they formed the independence government.

Independence and Growing Rivalries

Ugandans joyfully celebrated the independence of their nation on October 9, 1962. Uganda had very good prospects. It had rich farmland, a good climate, a booming economy, and a well-educated population. It had achieved independence without a bloody war. Beneath the calm surface, however, ethnic rivalries were simmering and threatening to come to a boil.

Milton Obote was the leader of the newly independent Uganda, but his power base was built on a shaky foundation. Each of his closest political appointees represented a different ethnic group, and each wanted more money and resources for his own territory than the country could deliver. Obote tried to accommodate everyone.

A year after he came to power, Obote faced a revolt by some units of the Ugandan army. They wanted better pay and the advancement of African military officers in the place of British officers. Obote turned to the British to help end the uprising. Although the soldiers opposed to Obote lost the battle, he gave in to all their demands.

Idi Amin, a Ugandan army officer, supported Obote. Amin was a powerful figure who had been trained by the British when Uganda was still a colony. Despite his limited education and belonging to a small ethnic group, the Kakwa, he quickly rose in the ranks.

Milton Obote served first as prime minister and later as president of Uganda.

The Obote Years

Obote sought political support from the Banyoro by working to regain the land they had lost to the Baganda. In 1964, he put this change to a vote. The Banyoro won, forcing the Baganda to give up the land. Tensions among ethnic groups grew stronger.

On February 4, 1966, the Ugandan parliament, the country's lawmaking body, voted to remove Obote from power. Instead of resigning, however, Obote used the army to take direct control of the government. He suspended the constitution, arrested officials who opposed him, and wrote his own constitution.

Uganda was now under martial law, meaning that the military kept

order. When the kabaka, Mutesa II, objected, Obote sent Amin and his troops to attack his palace. The kabaka managed to escape to Britain, never to return to Uganda. Obote brutally suppressed every opposition voice and clamped down on people's freedoms. Corruption became widespread as people tried to buy influence from anyone in power.

Amin and Obote competed for loyalty within the army. Amin himself became a threat to Obote rather than a supporter. Obote intended to fire Amin from his position as head of the army. Amin learned of the plan and used his loyal officers to seize power while Obote was out of the country in 1971. His troops attacked important targets in Kampala, the capital. They also attacked the airport at nearby Entebbe. They quickly ousted all Obote supporters who held important positions.

General Idi Amin speaks to reporters after taking control of Uganda in 1971.

The reign of Idi Amin has been recognized as one of the most brutal and erratic in Africa's history. Amin forced most Asians to leave Uganda. This pleased some Ugandans who resented the Asians' success. But Asian businesses were central to Uganda's economy, and without them, the economy quickly ground to a halt. Many of the Asians were British citizens, and they fled to England. Amin next ejected white British citizens from Uganda.

At first, many Ugandans supported Amin because they had been unhappy with Obote's oppressive rule. Amin's government was recognized by Britain and the United States. But President Julius Nyerere of Tanzania refused to accept the new government. Living in a neighboring country, he was aware of Amin's cruelty. Every time a group rose to oppose Amin, he attacked its members brutally. It is estimated that Amin's military police and death squads killed 300,000 people during his regime, which lasted from 1971 to 1979. Many people were tortured before they were killed.

Amin's regime ended when various Ugandan groups, banding together as the Uganda National Liberation Army, joined forces with the Tanzanian army and defeated Amin's soldiers. On April 11, 1979, liberation forces captured Kampala and Amin escaped to Saudi Arabia.

Obote Returns

The parties who had opposed Amin were poorly organized, and Milton Obote was able to regain the presidency by cheating in the election. Yoweri Museveni, the leader of a party called the Uganda Patriotic Movement, told Obote that if the election was dishonest, he would continue to fight. Museveni's National Resistance Army (NRA) fought a civil war throughout Obote's administration.

Corruption and brutality were widespread as Obote attempted to keep control. The Obote government forced an estimated 750,000 people to move from the Luwero District, in central Uganda, in an effort to stop them from aiding Museveni's soldiers. Obote's rule came to an end on July 27, 1985, when a faction of the Ugandan army overthrew him. Various factions continued to fight until they were defeated in 1987.

Yoweri Museveni became president of Uganda in 1986, after the country had experienced many years of violence and corruption.

Museveni Rules

In January 1986, Museveni took the oath of office as president. He inherited a nation that was physically and emotionally devastated. The agricultural and business bases of the nation had been destroyed. Most people, however, were hopeful and supported Museveni in his efforts to put things right again. He adopted policies that assured foreign investors their money would be safe. He encouraged tourism. Gradually, the economy grew.

Trouble in the North

Trouble remained, however, in the north. Both Obote's government and the factions that overthrew him had relied on northern soldiers. These soldiers regrouped to cause trouble. Near the northern border with Sudan, where the land is dry and life is hard, new rebel groups opposed to Museveni also emerged.

In 1986 and 1987, Alice Auma Lakwena led a rebel group called the Holy Spirit Movement. Lakwena convinced her "soldiers," who had no weapons, that they would be protected against bullets by the cooking oil she had them rub on their bodies. Even after many of them had been shot and killed, the others continued fighting until all were killed or captured. Lakwena escaped, however, and fled to neighboring Kenya, where she lived until her death in 2007.

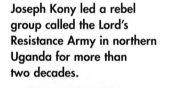

Joseph Kony led a rebel group called the Lord's Resistance Army in northern Uganda for more than two decades.

In 1987, a new rebel leader named Joseph Kony emerged in the north. Kony led a group called Lord's Resistance Army (LRA) and claimed he was fighting to replace the government of Uganda with one based on the Bible's Ten Commandments.

His "army" was composed of children whom he had kidnapped. He used fear and intimidation to turn them into soldiers. During the years that Kony and his soldiers held northern Uganda in their grip, Uganda's government forced about 1.7 million people from their homes into refugee camps in order to protect them from the LRA. This was most of the region's population.

In August 2008, Kony, who had been living in Sudan for several years,

Going Home

For the children who were kidnapped and forced to be soldiers in the Lord's Resistance Army, the road back to regular life is long. Agnes Ocitti was kidnapped from school in 1996. She was just 14 years old. She, other kidnapped children, and their kidnappers were constantly on the move through the wilderness, often living without any shelter. She finally managed to run away near the border with Sudan. When she was reunited with her parents and returned to a normal life, she resumed her education. Today, she is a human rights lawyer. She says, "I chose this job because I want to help those who—like me—are affected by the conflict."

fled into Congo with some of his troops, though LRA solders also remained in Uganda. Gradually, the people who had been displaced began returning home. But before they can farm and raise cattle again, they must repair the damage done to their land during the long war. In the meantime, they live in camps set up by international aid agencies. The camps provide food, water, shelter, and security.

Even in the middle of this tragedy, young people flock to the schools that have been set up within the camps. This thirst for education and ability to bounce back from tragedy are typical of Ugandans. They appear determined to make the most of the peace that has come to their country and to rebuild.

Ugandan refugees at a camp in northern Uganda watch an aircraft that is bringing food.

Governing Uganda

UGANDA IS MADE UP OF MANY DIFFERENT ETHNIC GROUPS and cultures, but Ugandans have come together to form a democratic society. Uganda is a republic, a nation in which the people elect representatives to govern according to law. The Ugandan government is divided into three parts: an executive branch, a legislative branch, and a judicial branch.

Opposite: **Members of the Ugandan government meet in Kampala.**

The Ugandan Parliament building is located in the heart of Kampala.

A Ugandan man casts his ballot in the 2006 presidential election.

NATIONAL GOVERNMENT OF UGANDA

Executive Branch

PRESIDENT

VICE PRESIDENT

CABINET MINISTERS

Legislative Branch

PARLIAMENT
(332 MEMBERS)

Judicial Branch

SUPREME COURT

COURTS OF APPEALS

HIGH COURTS

MAGISTRATE'S COURTS

The Executive Branch

The leader of the executive branch is the president, who is both the chief of state and the head of the government. The president is elected by popular vote. All citizens who are 18 or older are eligible to vote. The president serves a five-year term and can run for a second term.

In 2006, Parliament ended term limits at President Yoweri Museveni's request so that he could run for a third term. He won with 59 percent of the vote. The president appoints a vice president. He or she also appoints a cabinet of ministers, who head various government departments such as health, defense, and foreign affairs.

Yoweri Museveni

Yoweri Museveni has led the country during its most democratic period since the end of colonialism. Museveni was born in the western part of the country in 1944. He attended the University of Dar es Salaam in Tanzania, where he became politically active. He served under Ugandan president Milton Obote and fled the country in 1971 when Idi Amin seized power from Obote.

Museveni lived in Tanzania until 1979, when Amin was overthrown. That year, he returned to Uganda to become minister of defense. By 1981, he was the head of the National Resistance Army, which was trying to oust Obote. On January 26, 1986, he entered Kampala and, three days later, he took over as president. During the late 1980s, Museveni campaigned tirelessly to prevent the spread of AIDS. His policies lowered the rate of new infections dramatically.

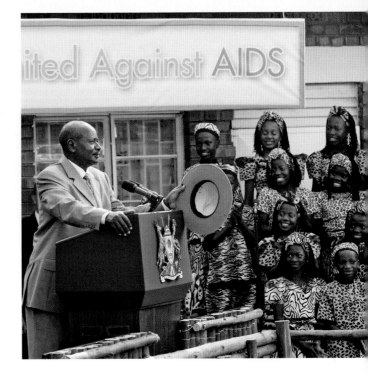

Princess and Diplomat

Princess Elizabeth of Toro (1936–) is the daughter of Rukidi III, the king of Toro. She attended elementary school in Uganda before her parents sent her to England for secondary school. She excelled in school and enrolled at Cambridge University, one of England's most prestigious schools, graduating in 1962 with a law degree. She was the first Ugandan woman to become a lawyer.

Throughout Uganda's tumultuous history, Elizabeth has been devoted to serving her country, though she has sometimes been forced into exile. After living in Europe for several years, in 1979 she returned to Uganda to help with the country's first free elections. In 1986, she became Uganda's ambassador to the United States and she later became the ambassador to Germany.

The National Flag

Uganda's flag features six horizontal stripes of equal size: two black, two yellow, and two red. Black represents Africa, yellow stands for sunshine, and red represents brotherhood. In the center of the flag is a white circle containing an image of the gray-crowned crane, the national bird of Uganda.

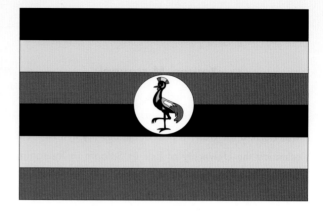

The National Anthem

George Wilberforce Kakomoa wrote the words and music to "Oh Uganda, Land of Beauty." In 1962, the song won a contest to become Uganda's national anthem.

Oh Uganda, land of beauty
Oh Uganda! May God uphold thee
We lay our future in thy hand.
United, free,
For liberty
Together we'll always stand.

Oh Uganda! The land of freedom
Our love and labor we give,
And with neighbors all
At our country's call
In peace and friendship we'll live.

Oh Uganda! The land that feeds us
By sun and fertile soil grown
For our own dear land,
We'll always stand,
The Pearl of Africa's Crown.

The Legislative Branch

Uganda's legislative branch of government is called Parliament. It has 332 members who serve five-year terms. Ugandans elect 215 of them from legislative districts. Other legislators are elected to represent various groups such as women, workers, members of the armed forces, youth, people with disabilities.

The Judicial Branch

Uganda's judicial system consists of magistrate's courts, high courts, courts of appeal, and the Supreme Court. Magistrate's courts handle minor cases. Major cases are heard in high courts. A high court decision can be reviewed by the court of appeal. The Supreme Court is the highest court in the land. It

In a court in Kampala, a man (right) stands trial for planning to overthrow the government.

reviews decisions made by the courts of appeals. Judges on the high courts, the courts of appeals, and the Supreme Court are all appointed by the president and approved by Parliament.

Local Government

Uganda is divided into 80 districts, which are subdivided into counties, subcounties, parishes, and villages. Districts receive funding from the national government to provide public services. They also raise money by taxing local residents.

Kampala: Did You Know This?

Kampala, the name of Uganda's capital city, means "Hill of Impalas" in the Baganda language. Impalas are graceful antelope that were kept by Kabaka Mutesa I, who ruled Buganda in the 19th century.

People of many ethnic groups live in Kampala, but the main group is the Baganda. Long before Uganda existed as a nation, Kampala served as the center of political life for the people of the Buganda Kingdom.

Today, Kampala is a modern city of 1.2 million people filled with lush parks and gardens. In recent years, it has also been filled with a growing number of cars and motorcycles called boda-bodas. People tear through the streets on boda-bodas, swerving through the traffic.

Kampala spreads out across a series of hills near Lake Victoria. Previous kabakas are buried

in the Kasubi Tombs on Kasubi Hill. The current kabaka's palace is located on Menga Hill.

Makerere Hill is the site of Makerere University. Kololo Hill features the Uganda National Museum, which includes displays on the culture, history, and natural history of the region. Other hills are home to the Kibuli Mosque, the Rubaga Catholic Cathedral, and the Namirembe Protestant Cathedral.

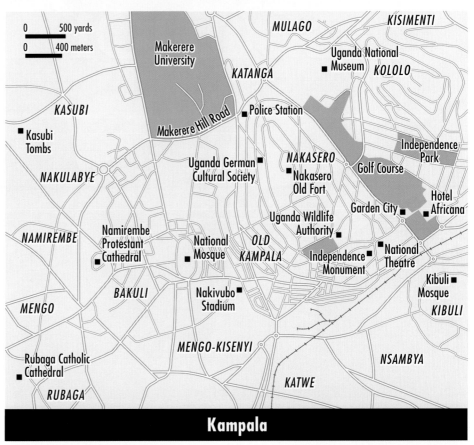

0 ⟶ 500 yards
0 ⟶ 400 meters

MULAGO

KISIMENTI

Makerere University

KATANGA

KASUBI

■ Kasubi Tombs

NAKULABYE

Makerere Hill Road

■ Police Station

Uganda National Museum ■

KOLOLO

Uganda German Cultural Society ■

NAKASERO

■ Nakasero Old Fort

Golf Course

Independence Park

Hotel Africana

Garden City ■

NAMIREMBE

Namirembe Protestant Cathedral ■

National Mosque ■

OLD KAMPALA

Uganda Wildlife Authority ■

Independence Monument ■

■ National Theatre

MENGO

BAKULI

Nakivubo Stadium ■

Kibuli ■ Mosque

KIBULI

Rubaga Catholic Cathedral ■

MENGO-KISENYI

NSAMBYA

RUBAGA

KATWE

Kampala

A Growing Economy

When Yoweri Museveni took over the government of Uganda in 1986, he inherited an economy that was in ruins, devastated by years of war and neglect. Much of the country's trade and business had been run by Asians, and when Idi Amin expelled them from Uganda and gave their businesses to his corrupt friends, the nation's economic base crumbled.

Immediately after taking office in 1986, Museveni announced a program to improve the economy. He worked to end corruption and to expand the nation's exports. He also invited Asians back to Uganda, promising that they could reclaim their property.

Many Asians returned to Uganda in the late 1980s and started over. One example is Sherali Bandali Jaffer, a man of Indian descent who was born in Uganda. Jaffer opened the Fairway Hotel in Kampala in the 1970s, just before he was forced to flee the country. Twenty years later, he responded to Museveni's offer, and the hotel was returned to him. He invested his own money

Opposite: **A Ugandan farmer picks a cabbage.**

Many pleasant resort hotels, such as the Lake Victoria Hotel in Entebbe, await visitors to Uganda.

in it, repairing the damage it had suffered during Uganda's war-torn years. Today, it is again a successful business.

Agriculture and Fishing

Agriculture is at the heart of the Ugandan economy. More than 80 percent of the population earns a living from farming, mostly on small-scale farms. People in rural areas grow their own food. Bananas are the most important crop. Cassava,

Below right: **Uganda is the second-largest banana producer, trailing only India.**

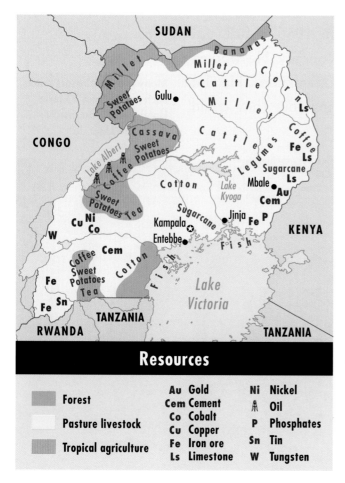

Resources

Forest	Au	Gold	Ni	Nickel
Pasture livestock	Cem	Cement	⚒	Oil
	Co	Cobalt	P	Phosphates
Tropical agriculture	Cu	Copper	Sn	Tin
	Fe	Iron ore	W	Tungsten
	Ls	Limestone		

sweet potatoes, millet, and legumes are other major crops. Coffee, the main agricultural export and the country's biggest cash earner, is grown in much of southern Uganda. Ugandans also grow tea and sugarcane for export.

Cotton was a major cash crop in Uganda during the colonial era. During the time when war rocked Uganda, the industry collapsed. But in recent years, cotton is again being produced in Uganda.

Workers pick tea leaves on a farm near Kampala. Uganda produces about 35,000 metric tons of tea per year.

What Uganda Grows, Makes, and Mines

Agriculture

Cattle (2001)	6,144,000 head
Coffee (2008)	168,000 metric tons
Cotton (2007)	13,000 metric tons

Manufacturing

Refined sugar (2008)	220,000 metric tons
Textiles (2003)	100,000 bales
Cigarettes	2,300,000,000 pieces

Mining

Gold (2005)	46 kilograms
Cobalt (2005)	638 metric tons
Limestone (2005)	540,756 metric tons

Ugandan fishers use a huge net to catch fish. About 1.5 million Ugandans make their living in the fishing industry.

Fishing is a key element in the country's economy. Fish exports brought in US$117 million in 2007. Nile perch and tilapia dominate the nation's fish exports.

Manufacturing

Uganda has begun to use its locally produced cotton to create a textile industry. TEXDA, the nation's textile development agency, was established in 1999 through a United Nations program working with the Ugandan government. It was set up to train local people in cotton production. At the TEXDA workshop in Kampala, fabrics are woven and dyed in traditional patterns. The company produces textiles for items such as curtains and tablecloths.

Uganda's textile industry shows off local talent in the annual Uganda International Fashion Week, held in November. The event brings together designers of fashion, fabric, and accessories. Ugandan designers combine traditional styles and designs with modern shapes, creating a uniquely African look. Most use 100 percent cotton fabrics, a legacy of Uganda's important cotton crop.

Manufacturing makes up only a small part of the Ugandan economy. Besides textiles, other important manufactured products are beverages, processed foods, and chemicals.

Miners drill through rock at the Kilembe Copper-Cobalt Mine in western Uganda.

Mining

Mining plays a minor role in the Ugandan economy. Resources mined in Uganda include gold, limestone, iron ore, and cobalt.

In 2006, oil was discovered in western Uganda, near Lake Albert. It is expected that these oil fields have reserves of between 100 million and 300 million barrels. As of 2009, development of the fields and construction of an oil refinery was just beginning. Many people expect oil to quickly become Uganda's main export.

Services

About 13 percent of Ugandans work in service industries. They work as teachers, bus drivers, and salespeople. But perhaps the most important service industry is tourism.

With its great natural beauty, its wildlife, and its growing number of hotels and lodges, Uganda is poised to become an important tourist destination. With peace, Ugandans have invested in building facilities in their national parks and improving transportation. Many Ugandans work as guides or in hotels or restaurants that cater to tourists. Visitors travel to Uganda to get a once-in-a-lifetime view of gorillas in the wild, to experience traditional cultures, or to race down rapids past jaw-dropping scenery.

A technician looks through a microscope at a health clinic. Health care workers are an important part of the service industry.

Changing Rivers

White-water rafting along a 30-mile (50 km) stretch of the Nile River starting just upriver from Bujagali Falls draws adventurous travelers. Uganda is rare among the nations of East Africa in welcoming backpackers, tourists who like to travel light and conserve their money. The road to the rapids is an adventure on its own. Travelers usually hop on motorbikes called boda-bodas, sitting behind the driver as the boda-boda bounces over the dirt road. Rapids are rated from one to five according to their difficulty. Some rapids on this stretch of the Nile are rated five, meaning they have large waves and hazards and only advanced rafters should try them.

In 2007, construction began on a dam just upriver from Bujagali Falls. The dam's generators are expected to double the amount of electricity produced in Uganda, enabling people to stop burning wood and

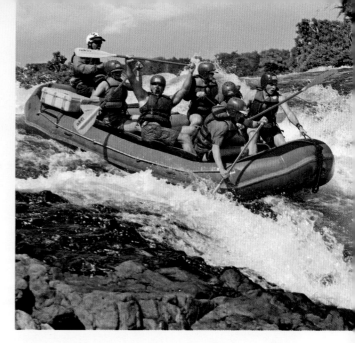

charcoal for cooking and heating water. Hundreds of families will have to move because their homes will be submerged by the lake created by the dam. And Bujagali Falls will disappear under the water. River rafters will still be able to run rapids, but they will have to do it farther upstream, away from the new dam.

Partly because of the growing tourist industry, Uganda has experienced a construction boom. In Kampala, many hotels have been built and other buildings have been renovated.

Transportation

About 44,000 miles (71,000 km) of roadways connect cities in Uganda, particularly in the south, but only about one-quarter of them are paved. The country's major international airport is at Entebbe, near Lake Victoria. Boats carry people and goods across Lake Victoria, Lake Albert, and Lake Kyoga. Lake Victoria's main ports are Port Bell and Jinja.

Cars and buses bump down a dirt road in Uganda. Nearly 80 percent of the nation's roads are unpaved.

Weights and Measures

Uganda uses the metric system of weights and measures. In this system, the basic unit of length is the meter; 1 meter is equal to 39.4 inches, or 3.3 feet. The basic unit of weight is the kilogram; 1 kilogram, or kilo, is equal to 2.2 pounds.

Northern Uganda remains the least developed part of the country. It is far from the capital and far from Lake Victoria, making transportation both difficult and expensive. For many years, road travel in the region was dangerous because of the rebel activity of the Lord's Resistance Army, which was fighting the Ugandan government. A civil war was also being fought in southern Sudan, Uganda's neighbor to the north. Now, with peace coming to both regions, Uganda and Sudan have signed an agreement to build a new railway line from Gulu in Uganda to Wau in Sudan. The Ugandan government is also working to upgrade existing roads in the region.

Communications

In Uganda and many other parts of Africa, telephone service was rare for a long time. Stringing landlines across remote deserts and mountains was expensive and difficult. When cell phone technology developed in the 1990s, African countries jumped at the opportunity. Cell phones did not require extensive wiring, especially in urban areas. As a result, cell phone usage boomed in Africa earlier than in the United States. In 2007, there were 4,195,000 cell phones in Uganda and just 162,300 landlines.

More than 4 million people in Uganda use cell phones.

Internet service is available in some areas, and the government is working on connecting all the major towns with high-speed lines.

Uganda has eight TV stations and several radio stations. Radio Uganda, the government-operated radio station, broadcasts in 24 languages. Major newspapers include *New Vision* and the *Monitor*.

Currency

Uganda's currency is called the shilling. Bills come in values of 1,000, 5,000, 10,000, 20,000, and 50,000 shillings. Coins are valued at 100, 200, and 500 shillings. Ugandan bills feature images of people and things important to Ugandan culture. For example, the 1,000-shilling note depicts a farmer, and the 20,000-shilling note shows a gray-crowned crane, the national bird. In 2009, 1 U.S. dollar was equal to 2,000 shillings.

The People of Uganda

UGANDA IS HOME TO ABOUT 31 MILLION PEOPLE. ONLY about 12 percent of them live in cities. The rest are spread across the country in small communities.

Uganda's people fall into more than 40 distinct cultural groups, each with its own language. These various ethnic communities can be divided into two large groups, the Bantu and the Nilotic peoples. The Bantu live mainly in the southern part of Uganda, and most Nilotic people live farther north. The term *Nilotic* comes from the Nile River. In Uganda, most people are Bantu.

Ethnic Groups

The largest ethnic group in the country, the Baganda, are Bantu. Buganda, the homeland of the Baganda, occupies much of central Uganda, wrapping around Lake Victoria and continuing northward. Its people trace their ancestry to a leader known as Kintu. Different stories tell how Kintu came to Buganda. Some people believe that

Opposite: **A woman and child from the Kayunga District, in central Uganda**

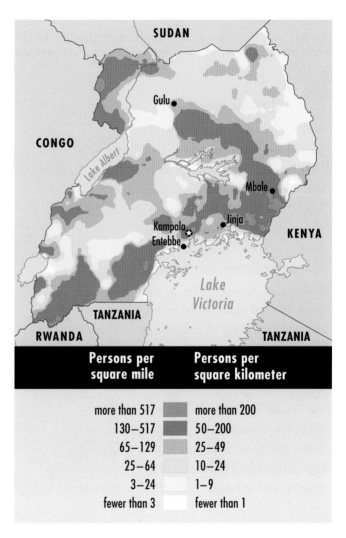

Persons per square mile	Persons per square kilometer
more than 517	more than 200
130–517	50–200
65–129	25–49
25–64	10–24
3–24	1–9
fewer than 3	fewer than 1

Kintu was a real person who established the Baganda Kingdom around 1300. For others, he is a mythical figure who represents the origin of all people on Earth.

The Baganda make up 17 percent of the Ugandan population. Their culture became dominant in Uganda in the 1800s. They have strong family ties and strong loyalty to their traditional leader, the kabaka. The Baganda also have strong self-discipline, believe in sharing one's wealth, and have a keen sense of hospitality.

Kasubi Tombs

Burying the kabaka is an important part of the Baganda culture. Each king was buried at his own shrine until the time of Mutesa I, who ruled from 1856 to 1884. He and the three kabakas who ruled after him are buried at Kasubi, now an important site near Kampala. The main building at Kasubi is the largest grass-thatched house in the nation. Its arches are made of palm leaves that are intricately woven. The tomb has 52 rings made of elephant grass that represent the clans of Buganda. The Kasubi Tombs are looked after by female descendants of the kings. When the body of Mutesa II was brought back from England in 1971, it was buried at Kasubi.

A Baganda man plays a traditional fiddle.

Who Lives in Uganda?

Baganda	17%
Ankole	8%
Basoga	8%
Iteso	8%
Bakiga	7%
Langi	6%
Rwanda	6%
Bagisu	5%
Acholi	4%
Lugbara	4%
Batoro	3%
Banyoro	3%
Alur	2%
Bakonjo	2%
Bgwere	2%
Jopodhola	2%
Karamojong	2%
Rundi	2%
European, Asian, and Arab	1%
Other	8%

Other major Bantu groups include the Ankole, the Basoga, and the Bakiga. All these groups live in the southern part of the country.

The largest Nilotic groups include the Langi and the Acholi. Most Nilotic peoples live in northern Uganda. The Karamojong live in the extreme northeastern part of the country, far from the capital and other major cities. In many ways, they live much as their ancestors did. Cattle herding is central to their culture. Karamojong women are noted for

Above: **A young Karamojong woman carries wood back to her village. She has scarification marks on the side of her face.**

their intricate scarification. They make patterns in their skin with tiny cuts that become scars. They consider the patterns a sign of beauty.

The largest group of people in Uganda who are not of African descent are South Asians. They are the descendants of people who came to Uganda in the 19th and 20th centuries. At one time, Uganda's Asian population numbered more than 50,000. Nearly all of them were expelled from the country in 1972, during Idi Amin's rule. In the 1990s, the Ugandan government invited Asians to return. Today, more than 15,000 Asians again live in Uganda.

Uganda has also served as a refuge for people escaping war in neighboring countries. The numbers shift frequently, but in 2008, for example, Uganda hosted more than 200,000 refugees, most of them from Sudan, Congo, and Rwanda.

Languages

Uganda has two official languages, English and Swahili. English is the language used in most schools. Swahili, which became an official language in 2005, is often used in trade. At least 20 languages can be heard on radio broadcasts in different parts of Uganda.

Thousands of refugees from Congo entered Uganda in late 2008, fleeing violence in their own country. Here, Congolese refugees wait for food to be handed out.

Luganda Terms

oliotya	hello
weraba	good-bye
webale	thank you
bambi	please
ye	yes
neda	no

Luganda, the language of the Baganda, is spoken by more than 10 million people. Luganda is a tonal language. In tonal languages, changing a word's pitch can change its meaning. For example, *kabaka* means "king" if all three syllables have the same pitch. But if the first syllable has a high pitch, the meaning of the word changes to a version of the verb *to catch*. Because of this, Luganda is a difficult language for outsiders to learn.

Education

Formal education has been important in Uganda since missionaries first arrived in the 1800s. School attendance is not required, yet 87 percent of primary school-aged children are

A Ugandan teacher explains an assignment to students.

enrolled in school. The war years were devastating to the nation's education system. The nation was desperately in need of teachers and schools. When Yoweri Museveni became president in 1986, he made literacy a national goal. School buildings were renovated and teaching standards were raised. Students were encouraged to stay in school beyond the primary grades. More schools offered technical and vocation training.

In less than 10 years, the number of children attending primary school had doubled.

In 1996, Museveni introduced free primary education for all children. This was a bold and effective move. The number of children attending school increased dramatically. Today, about 67 percent of Ugandan adults can read and write.

Makerere University, which was founded in 1922 in Kampala, is the nation's largest university. Smaller schools include the Uganda Martyrs University and Ndejje University, both in Kampala; Uganda Christian University, in Mukono; the Mbarara University of Science and Technology, in Mbarara; and the Islamic University, in Mbale.

The department of Computing and Information Technology is based in a new building at Makerere Univeristy. About 30,000 students attend the university.

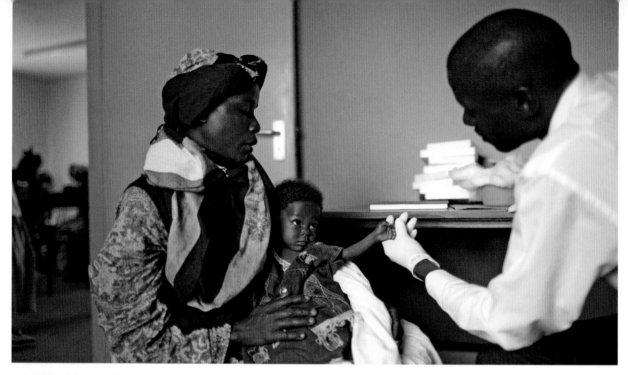

A health center worker examines a mother and child. Because of the ravages of diseases such as AIDS and malaria, men in Uganda live an average of just 47 years and women an average of 50 years.

Health Care

Many nations in Africa have been devastated by AIDS, an often fatal disease caused by a virus called HIV. While some nations have been slow to respond to the crisis, Uganda has not. President Museveni's government began a program that educated people about how to prevent the spread of AIDS. When Museveni became president, Uganda had one of the highest rates of HIV infection in the world. Now, thanks to the forthright and open campaign to help people avoid getting AIDS, the rate of new infections has fallen dramatically, and Uganda is considered a success story.

Another major threat in Uganda is malaria, the number-one killer on the continent. Malaria is a disease that causes fevers, chills, and nausea. It is spread by bites from infected mosquitoes. Although it is possible to treat malaria, the best way to deal with the disease is to prevent it. Mosquito

Caring for Uganda's Orphans

An estimated 2 million children in Uganda have lost their parents to war and disease. Private charities have stepped in to help where they can.

The Rotary Club of Kololo constructed a building to take care of sick children. Rotarian Mukasa Sam Farouk, who makes his living in a company that sells machinery, is proud of the work of his group. "We presently cater for an average of 90 children at any one time in our Nguru reception center."

In 2009, a team of four marathoners took on the cause of Uganda's orphans. They ran seven marathons in seven days on seven continents. They raised US$200,000 to support Isaac's House, an orphanage in Entebbe. The worldwide attention to their effort shows how individuals can help Uganda cope with the needs of its many orphans.

bites can be prevented by sleeping beneath netting that has been treated with insecticide that kills the bugs. In Uganda, an estimated 12 million people are sickened by malaria each year. Children are most likely to die from the disease. An estimated 70,000 to 100,000 Ugandan children die from malaria every year.

Mosquito netting is a vital tool in the fight against malaria.

Now, an organization called "Nothing but Nets" is working to provide insecticide-treated mosquito nets to hundreds of thousands of refugees living in camps in Uganda and elsewhere in East Africa. The need is greatest during the rainy season, when the mosquitoes breed and multiply. One mosquito net can protect a family of four people.

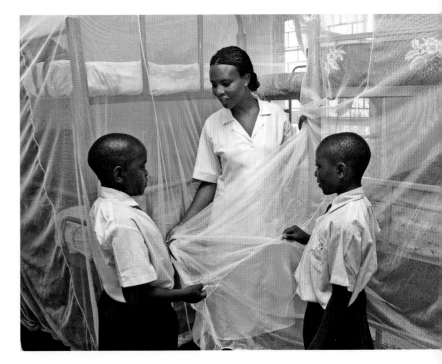

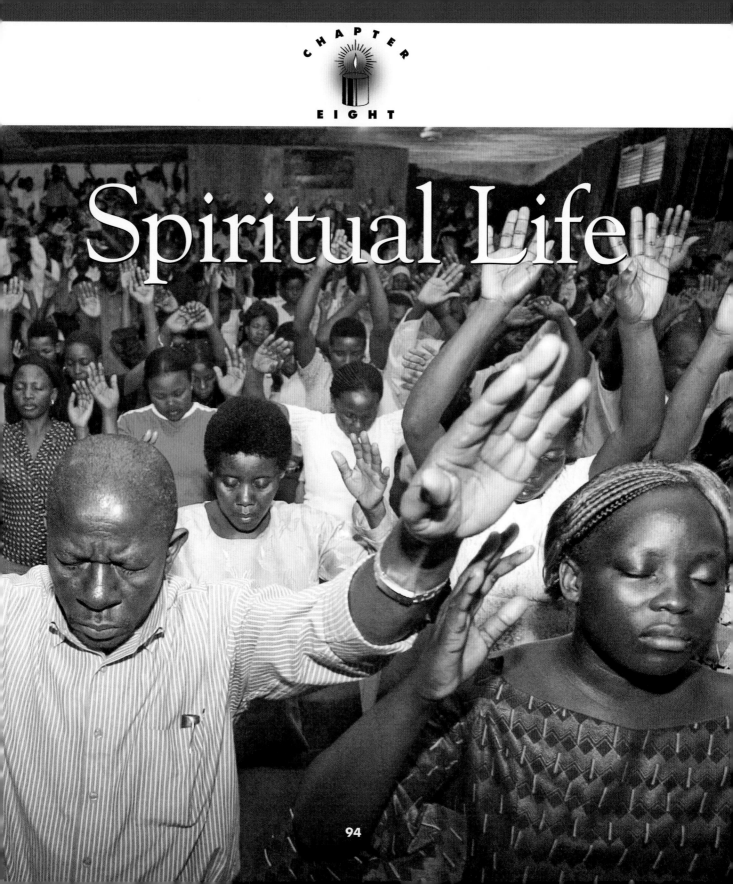

CHAPTER

EIGHT

Spiritual Life

The Baha'i House of Worship is located in Kampala. About 100,000 Ugandans belong to the Baha'i faith.

W HEN EUROPEAN MISSIONARIES FIRST ARRIVED IN Uganda, they found a population with well-established, traditional religious beliefs. In traditional Ugandan religions, people believe in a power larger and stronger than themselves. This power can be found throughout the natural world. People communicate with this power through dreams and visions or through people with special abilities to make contact with the higher power. Today, many Ugandans combine Christian religious beliefs with traditional religious beliefs.

Opposite: **Worshippers raise their hands in prayer at a Pentecostal church in Kampala. Pentecostals are the fastest-growing religious group in Uganda.**

Catholic Ugandans touch a
wooden crucifix as part of
the national Martyrs' Day
holiday.

Christianity

Christian missionaries, both Protestant and Catholic, arrived
in Uganda in the 19th century. They worked to convert
Ugandans to their particular belief systems. People were
taught Christian beliefs and practices and urged to give up
their traditional beliefs.

Today, about 42 percent of Ugandans are Roman Catholic,
and about 42 percent belong to various Protestant groups.
The largest Protestant group is Anglicans. Other major groups
include Pentecostals and Seventh-day Adventists.

Islam

The first outside religion introduced in Uganda was Islam, which came to the region around 1844 from East Africa. When Kabaka Mutesa I converted to Islam, the religion gained many converts among the Baganda. The religion grew, particularly in the north, which is closest to North Africa, where Islam is the dominant religion.

Muslims in Uganda generally set themselves apart from people of other religions by their dress. Both women and men wear long, loose outer garments that provide modesty by covering their bodies. As girls grow older, they cover their hair with a headscarf. After they marry, many also cover their faces.

Religions in Uganda

Catholicism	42%
Protestantism	42%
Islam	12%
Other	4%

Muslim children gather for prayer in Kampala.

The Five Pillars of Islam

Muslims follow five basic principles called the Five Pillars of Islam. They form the backbone of the faith.

1. *Shahada* is a statement of faith in which Muslims declare, "There is no god but God, and Muhammad is his messenger."
2. *Salat* is prayer. Muslims pray five times a day.
3. *Zakat* is giving to charity. Muslims should give generously to the poor.
4. *Sawm* is fasting, or going without food. Muslims fast during Ramadan, the ninth month of the Muslim calendar.
5. The *hajj* is a pilgrimage. If they are physically and financially able, Muslims make a journey to Mecca, Saudi Arabia, the holiest city in Islam, at least once in their lifetime.

Muslims pray at a mosque in Kampala. During prayer, Muslims bow in the direction of Mecca, Saudi Arabia, the holiest city in Islam.

Ramadan is the holiest month in the Muslim calendar. Each day during Ramadan, Muslims fast from sunup to sundown. They believe that fasting cleanses them spiritually and makes them more compassionate toward the poor. At the end of Ramadan, Muslims celebrate a festival called 'Id al-Fitr, the "Breaking of the Fast." This is a joyous time that involves special prayers, lavish family meals, and gifts for children.

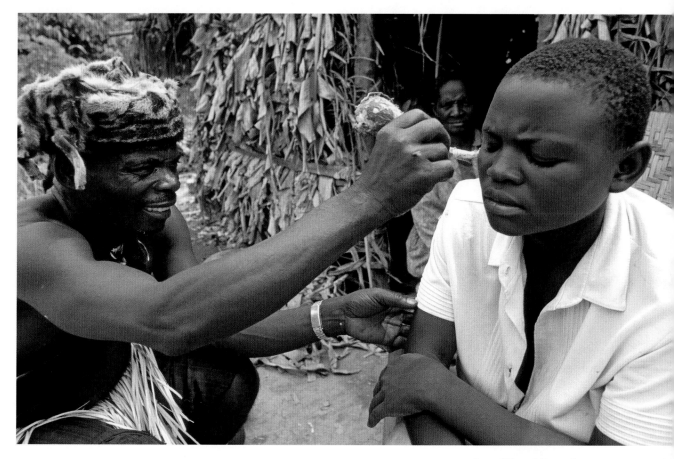

A traditional Ugandan
healer works on a patient.

Traditional Religions

About 86 percent of Ugandans are Christian and about 12 percent are Muslim, but many also still hold some traditional beliefs. Traditional religions help a person fit into the community. They give people a sense of their place in society by tying them together with their ancestors as well as with their living relatives. They also help people settle disputes through compromise and ease their suffering as a result of disease or the loss of a loved one.

Ugandans sometimes enter trances during traditional religious ceremonies.

In southern Uganda, people offer prayers and sacrifices to show respect for the dead. In western Uganda, people who follow the Mbandwa religion sometimes use trances and prayer to ask the spirit world to help the living.

In northwestern Uganda, the Lugbara people pay close attention to the spirits of their ancestors, believing that they communicate directly with the living and play a role in whether they have good or bad fortune. Elders also receive great respect and carry great influence. They keep shrines where they communicate with ancestral spirits. Because spirits are believed to be able to put a curse on someone, people often visit elders to find out if a spirit caused an illness.

Among the Baganda, the importance of the kabaka, their traditional king, is tied up with religious beliefs. The kabaka acts to protect the kingdom from evil spiritual forces. Traditional people worship gods that they believe are responsible for events such as rain, drought, lightning, and illness. Following these beliefs, people make sacrifices to the gods to ensure good hunting and good health.

Kabaka Mutebi II

Ronald Muwenda Mutebi II, the 36th kabaka of Buganda, was crowned on July 31, 1993, in a traditional ceremony attended by President Yoweri Museveni. Mutebi II knew that he would be the next kabaka from the time he was 14, when his father died in exile in London. Mutebi did not return to Uganda until 1986, after Museveni took over the government. To the Baganda, the kabaka remained the most important figure even when he was not present in Uganda. One man summed it all up by saying, "The kabaka is in our blood."

CHAPTER NINE

Arts, Music, and Sports

102

I N TRADITIONAL UGANDAN COMMUNITIES, PEOPLE MADE every object they needed in their everyday life by hand. They took care to make these objects in the most beautiful way, with a pleasing appearance.

Opposite: **Children drum and clap at a dance performance.**

Traditional Crafts

Handcrafted items made in Uganda include gourds, which were used to prepare and serve food and drinks. Gourds grow naturally in a variety of shapes and sizes, from tiny ones, which can be used to hold a single serving of food, to giant ones, which can be used to mix up enough porridge to feed

Basket weaving has a long tradition in Uganda. Here, women in Mbarara in the southwestern part of the country show off spectacular baskets.

an entire family. People sometimes etched the gourds' tough outer skin with a design. They also smoked the gourds, which sealed them so that they could hold liquids.

Weavers made baskets out of tree fibers, while potters used clay to shape pots that were fired and used for cooking. Ugandan basketry is known for its distinctive, fine weave and its varied patterns and colors. Finely made baskets are now considered works of art and are purchased by people as decorative objects. Besides baskets, Ugandans also wove fences and animal traps.

A potter fashions large cooking pots in Muku, in southwestern Uganda. Most potters in Uganda are male.

Before Europeans introduced cotton and other fabrics, the Bantu people of Uganda made cloth pounded from the bark of the fig tree. They used this material for bedding and clothing as well as for carpeting in the kings' palaces. Eventually, cotton cloth replaced bark cloth.

Traditionally, children learned craft skills from their parents and other elders. Boys and girls learned different skills that they would need in their adult lives. Men made bark cloth, while women wove baskets. When missionaries arrived in the 19th century, they introduced reading and writing,

Fabrics with bold patterns are common in Uganda. Here, aid workers present new beds in a village in northern Uganda.

particularly to boys. As time went on, only girls and women made household products.

Opposite: **Ugandan drums come in many shapes and sizes.**

Drums

Dances are at the heart of Buganda culture. They play an important role in the ceremonies of Uganda's many ethnic groups. They communicate cultural ideas and history. Drums are made in a wide variety of shapes and materials that enable musicians to produce many tones and moods. Some drums are used only to announce the birth of a royal child and proclaim the installation of a king.

Long before there were cell phones, drums were a vital means of communication. Different rhythms, pounded out on a "talking drum" called *ngoma*, were used to let members of the group know that they were needed. Each rhythm told a different message: one said that a group was needed to hunt; another, that there was danger coming from outside the group; yet another rhythm let members know they were needed for a communal work activity. Children learned to understand these messages at an early age. Even today, in some rural areas, drums are used to tell people they are needed to work in the fields or repair roads.

The Uganda National Museum

The Uganda National Museum, which opened in Kampala in 1908, is filled with exhibits detailing the cultures of Uganda. On display are many musical instruments native to Uganda, including early flutes, harps, and talking drums. Sometimes, people demonstrate how to play the instruments. Museum displays also depict traditional crafts, farming skills, and other aspects of Ugandan culture.

Dance is at the heart of the culture of many of Uganda's ethnic groups. Each group has created its own dance rituals, which are a way to worship, to praise, and to celebrate the cycle of life. Dance is also a form of community recreation.

Dancers perform at the enthronement ceremony of Kabaka Mutebi II.

The *bwola* dance of the Acholi is performed before the chief, usually at his installation. It is also danced at the chief's death. The drum used to accompany the dance is also called the bwola. The dancers are arranged in two circles, with women on the inner circle and men on the outer circle. The two circles move in opposite directions. The Acholi also perform the *larakaraka*, a courtship dance, and the *lukeme*, a competitive dance.

A group of Karamojong people begin a dance. Each ethnic group in Uganda has its own dances.

The Spirit of Uganda group rehearses before a 2008 performance in New York City.

Among the Lugbara people, the *nambi* is a traditional marriage dance. It is a very fast dance, and young people put all their energy into it.

The Alur people dance the *adungu*, which is also the name of a bow harp. It is a fast social dance, full of quick movements. The Iteso people perform the *akogo*. For men, this is a vigorous, athletic dance, while for women, it mostly involves upper-body movements.

All these dances and dozens of others are passed down from generation to generation, helping preserve the cultures of the various groups.

Many modern Ugandan dance groups, such as Infinity, incorporate traditional movements in their work but add their own interpretations. The Spirit of Uganda is a group of 22 young performers, aged 8 to 18, who have been orphaned by disease or war. The children tour the United States every two years, using song, dance, and music to describe their cultures.

Art

Expedito Kibbula, one of Uganda's most renowned artists, makes dramatic metal sculptures. *Universal Couple* is a sculpture of two narrow, angular figures embracing that stands 5 feet (1.5 m) tall. Like many Ugandan artists, Kibbula studied art at Makerere University. "Art school was important because you were exposed to the wider school of society and the environment, mingling with architects, lawyers, doctors, and many other people," he says.

Cricket is a popular sport in Uganda. Here, Uganda's Joel Olwenyi plays in a match against Bangladesh.

The work of many Ugandan artists reflects their country's history. Ignatius Sserulyo makes large paintings that depict traditional Ugandan stories. Artist Francis Nnaggenda's massive sculptures honor Ugandans' spirit in the face of adversity. His sculpture titled *War Victim* recalls the horrors that Ugandans suffered in the 1970s and 1980s.

Sports

Soccer is the most popular sport in Uganda. Children play the game on any kind of field they can find, even in the heart of Kampala with office buildings looming in the background. Basketball is also popular, as are tennis, cricket, volleyball, and rugby.

Ugandan David Obua (in red) and Nigerian Obafemi Martins fight for the ball during a match in 2007.

Uganda sent 22 athletes to the Summer Olympic Games in 2008. Most of them were track-and-field athletes. They included Dorcus Inzikuru, the 2005 world champion in the women's steeplechase. She did not win a medal in the 2008 Olympics, but she represented her country proudly. As of 2008, Ugandan athletes had won a total of six Olympic medals, four in boxing and two in track-and-field events.

Dorcus Inzikuru waves after winning a 3,000-meter steeplechase race.

One of the most inspiring athletes in Uganda is Bashir Ramathan. Though he is blind, he competes as a middle-weight boxer, serving as a bold model to Uganda's half-million blind citizens.

Bashir Ramathan trains at a Kampala gym in 2007.

CHAPTER TEN

Daily Life

Some people in rural Uganda continue to rely on ancient traditions. During dry times, people may call in a medicine man, called an *emurron*, to preside over a rainmaking ceremony. When the emurron comes to ask the rain to fall, the clan slaughters and cooks a bull. The elders of the clan eat the meat, but the emurron is given an entire leg as thanks for his service.

Opposite: **A Ugandan family eats breakfast outside of their home.**

In Uganda, traditional religious ceremonies sometimes include feasts.

Marriage and Family

In traditional Ugandan cultures in the past, before two people got married they had to ask elders for permission to wed. The groom also provided money to the family of the bride. This tradition continues to this day, although the payment may be something symbolic, such as a Bible. In Baganda society, a groom must write a letter to his future bride's family, expressing his understanding of his financial obligations to them. The letter must be written perfectly in Luganda, the language of the Baganda. Some people hire professional letter writers to do the job. They want to make sure they establish a good relationship with their future in-laws.

Wedding Photos

Every Saturday afternoon, as many as a dozen or more wedding parties come to the grounds of the Sheraton Hotel to have their photographs taken. The bride and groom are positioned in a lovely place in the garden.

In Kampala, many Ugandans have Western-style Christian weddings. The bride wears an elaborate white wedding dress, and the groom wears a suit. The bride's many attendants wear matching gowns.

Ugandans tend to have large families, and many Ugandans are young. More than 50 percent of the Ugandan population is under the age of 15, the highest percentage in the world. Women have an average of 6.8 children.

Before they marry, Ugandans talk to their parents about raising children. Aunts and uncles often play important roles in bringing up children. All children are taught to address older people with respect. Baganda children are taught how to behave properly within their community, but many of them are eventually sent away from home to live with others, to learn how to live in the larger society.

In Uganda, members of the extended family often help raise children and instruct them about proper behavior.

Some rural women wear basuuti, the Ugandan traditional dress. Here, women balance baskets filled with potatoes on top of their heads.

Ugandan Dress

In Uganda's large cities, women wearing the *basuuti*, the national dress of Uganda, walk alongside other women wearing Western-style dress. The basuuti is a long, brightly colored dress of printed fabric. A belt or sash called a *kitambaala* holds the dress in place. The number of Ugandan women who wear traditional clothes is falling. As people move to the city or enter business, they often adopt Western styles.

Men also wear Western-style clothing, although they sometimes wear traditional clothing at ceremonies. Traditional dress for Baganda men includes a long white robe called a *kanzu*, which they sometimes wear under a jacket.

A father wearing traditional clothing heads out to the fields with his son.

Royal Ascot Goat Race

One of the biggest social events of the year in Kampala is the Royal Ascot Goat Race, which is patterned on the Ascot horse race in England. The event is held on the grounds of the Royal Speke Resort in Munyonyo, on the shore of Lake Victoria. It is a day of fun, food, fashion, entertainment, and, of course, goat races. Goats are not easy to herd, so much of the "racing" consists of the goats' owners pushing their animals. Prizes are awarded for the best costumes. Entertainment includes traditional and modern dance exhibitions and a fireworks display. The event raises money for charities that help the blind and others in need.

A woman walks near her home in eastern Uganda. Most Ugandans live in villages where the homes are made of natural materials such as mud and grass.

Village Life

In Ugandan villages, most people raise cattle and crops. In the most rural areas, they build houses from mud, using bundles of grass for roofing. In some villages, people find different building materials. They might build houses from reeds and sticks and use corrugated iron for roofs. These kinds of houses are usually larger than houses made from mud. The houses are often home to 12 or more people.

A woman collects water from a pool near the city of Soroti.

Typically, rural Ugandans cook over an open fire in a smaller building near the main house. Over time, smoke from the cooking fire stains the walls of the building. Rural houses do not having running water. People collect water from a stream or a well and carry it back to the house in large plastic jugs called jerry cans. Sometimes they use clay pots.

Uganda's main foods are plantains, cassavas, sweet potatoes, millet, sorghum, corn, beans, and peanuts.

Many main dishes start with a sauce or stew made with peanuts, beans, or meat. Boiled greens are sometimes included in the stews. This is accompanied by *ugali*, a thick porridge made from cornmeal. *Matoke*, a kind of banana that is boiled and then mashed, is also popular.

Ugandans who can afford it eat chicken, fish, beef, goat, and mutton on a daily basis. In many rural areas, however, it is rare to slaughter a valuable large animal. In these places, people eat meat only at important ceremonies.

This typical stew is made up of potatoes, cabbage, and beans.

Playing Oware

Oware, which is also known by names such as *man-cala* and *wari*, is the most popular game in Africa. It is a two-person board game. The board contains a total of 12, 24, or 36 cups arranged in rows. At the end of the board are 2 extra cups. These hold each player's game pieces, which are often pebbles, seeds, or whatever else is handy. If no one has a board, players may scratch one in the sand.

At the start of the game, 4 pieces are placed in each of the 12 cups. To start, a player picks up all the pieces in 1 cup in his or her own row and moves around the board, depositing 1 piece in each cup until the pieces are used up. The other player then does the same. Play continues until one player has accumulated all the other's pieces.

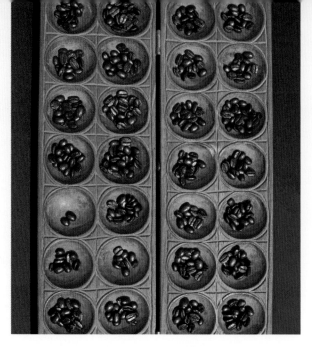

Though the game has simple rules, playing it well requires an understanding of mathematics. Players sometimes go so fast, you can hardly see their pieces move.

National Holidays

New Year's Day	January 1
Liberation Day	January 26
Good Friday	March or April
Easter Monday	March or April
Labor Day	May 1
Martyrs' Day	June 3
National Heroes' Day	June 9
Independence Day	October 9
Christmas	December 25
Boxing Day	December 26
'Id al-Fitr (End of Ramadan)	varies
'Id al-Adha (Feast of the Sacrifice)	varies

Into the Future

The people of Uganda are cautiously optimistic about the future of their country. Every day, they see improvements. In the war-torn north, people are hopeful that peace agreements will hold, allowing the region to return to normal. Foreign investors are bringing in money, boosting Uganda's economy.

Across the country, many young people identify themselves by their nationality rather than by their ethnic background. They are coming together as one people. They are Ugandans.

Uganda has experienced great trauma though the decades, but most Ugandans maintain a positive view of life.

Timeline

Ugandan History		World History	
		c. 3000 BCE	Forms of writing are invented in China, India, and Sumeria.
		c. 2500 BCE	Egyptians build pyramids in Giza.
Bantu and Nilotic people migrate to region.	**c. 1000** CE	**c. 563** BCE	The Buddha is born in India.
		c. 469 BCE	Socrates is born in Greece.
		313 CE	Roman emperor Constantine recognizes Christianity.
		610	The Prophet Muhammad begins preaching Islam.
		618–907	The Tang dynasty rules China.
		1206–1227	Genghis Khan rules the Mongol Empire.
		1215	King John of England agrees to the Magna Carta.
		1300s	The Renaissance begins in Italy.
		1400s	The Inca flourish in the Andes, and the Aztec thrive in what is now Mexico.
		1464	The Songhay Empire is established in West Africa.
		1492	Christopher Columbus arrives in the Americas.
		1502	Enslaved Africans are first brought to the Americas.
		1517	The Protestant Reformation begins.
		1776	Americans sign the Declaration of Independence.
		1804	Haiti becomes independent following the only successful slave uprising in history.
		1823	The United States announces the Monroe Doctrine.
Arab traders reach Buganda; Islam is introduced.	1844	1861–1865	American Civil War
John Hanning Speke discovers a source of the Nile River.	1862		
Members of the Church Missionary Society of London arrive in Buganda.	1877		
French Catholic missionaries arrive in Buganda.	1879		

Ugandan History

At the Berlin Conference, European powers divide Africa among themselves; Great Britain acquires what is now Uganda.	**1884–1885**
Britain declares a protectorate over Buganda, beginning colonial rule there.	**1894**
Bunyoro, Toro, and Ankole are added to the British protectorate.	**1896**
Makerere University is founded as a technical school. It is the first institution of higher learning in East Africa.	**1922**
More than 75,000 Ugandans fight with the British in World War II.	**1939–1945**
Anti-British riots break out, as the Baganda demand greater economic and political participation in Uganda's affairs.	**1949**
Uganda gains independence from Great Britain; Milton Obote becomes Uganda's first prime minister.	**1962**
Idi Amin seizes power; corruption and brutality mark his reign.	**1971**
Amin orders all Asians to leave Uganda.	**1972**
Liberation forces oust Amin; Obote returns to power.	**1979**
Yoweri Museveni's National Resistance Army takes Kampala; Museveni becomes president.	**1986**
Joseph Kony forms a rebel movement called the Lord's Resistance Army (LRA) in northern Uganda.	**1987**
Oil is discovered in western Uganda.	**2006**

World History

1914–1918	World War I
1917	The Bolshevik Revolution brings communism to Russia.
1929	A worldwide economic depression sets in.
1939–1945	World War II
1950s–1960s	African colonies win independence from European nations.
1957–1975	Vietnam War
1989	The cold war ends as communism crumbles in Eastern Europe.
1994	South Africa abolishes apartheid.
2001	Terrorists attack the World Trade Center in New York City and the Pentagon in Arlington, Virginia.
2004	A tsunami in the Indian Ocean destroys coastlines in Africa, India, and Southeast Asia.
2008	The United States elects its first African American president.

Fast Facts

Official name: Republic of Uganda

Capital: Kampala

Official languages: English, Swahili

Kampala

Uganda's flag

Rwenzori Mountains

Official religion:	None
Year of founding:	1962
National anthem:	"Oh Uganda, Land of Beauty"
Type of government:	Republic
Chief of state:	President
Head of government:	President
Area of country:	91,134 square miles (236,037 sq km)
Latitude and longitude of geographic center:	0° (equator), 32° E
Bordering countries:	Tanzania and Rwanda to the south, Congo to the west, Sudan to the north, and Kenya to the east
Highest elevation:	Margherita Peak on Mount Stanley, 16,763 feet (5,109 m)
Lowest elevation:	Lake Albert, 2,037 feet (621 m)
Average high temperatures:	In Kampala, 82°F (28°C) in January and 77°F (25°C) in July
Average low temperatures:	In Kampala, 64°F (18°C) in January and 63°F (17°C) in July
Average precipitation:	80 inches (200 cm) in the south, 20 inches (50 cm) in the north
National population (2007 est.):	30,900,000

Makerere University

Currency

Population of major cities (2002):

Kampala	1.2 million
Gulu	119,000
Jinja	86,000
Mbale	70,000

Landmarks:
- ▶ *Bwindi Impenetrable Forest National Park,* Kabale
- ▶ *Kasubi Tombs,* Kampala
- ▶ *Makerere University,* Kampala
- ▶ *Murchison Falls National Park,* Masindi
- ▶ *Uganda National Museum,* Kampala

Economy: Uganda's economy depends on agriculture. Bananas, cassava, and sweet potatoes are grown for consumption at home. Coffee, tea, and sugarcane are the major agricultural exports, with vegetables and cut flowers growing in importance. Fish is also an important export, particularly Nile perch and tilapia. Cotton is grown and turned into textiles. Beverages, processed foods, and chemicals are also produced. Gold, limestone, iron ore, and cobalt are mined, and oil has been discovered in the western part of the country. Tourism is the most important part of the service sector.

Currency: The Uganda shilling. In 2009, 1 U.S. dollar was equal to 2,000 shillings.

Weights and measures: Metric system

Literacy rate: 67%

Schoolchildren

Lugandan words and phrases:

oliotya	hello
weraba	good-bye
webale	thank you
bambi	please
ye	yes
neda	no
lero	today
enkya	tomorrow

Notable Ugandans:

Idi Amin Dada *Dictator*	(1925–2003)
Princess Elizabeth of Toro *Diplomat*	(1936–)
Dorcus Inzikuru *Athlete*	(1982–)
Yoweri Museveni *President*	(1944–)
Kabaka Mutesa I *King*	(1838–1884)
Kabaka Mutesa II *King*	(c. 1936–1969)
Okot p'Bitek *Poet*	(1931–1982)

Yoweri Museveni

To Find Out More

Books

▶ Appe, James. *Stories from Uganda*. Chicago: Heinemann, 2002.

▶ McDonnell, Faith J. H., and Grace Akallo. *Girl Soldier: A Story of Hope for Northern Uganda's Children*. Grand Rapids, Mich.: Baker Publishing Group, 2007.

▶ Otiso, Kefa M. *Culture and Customs of Uganda*. Westport, Conn.: Greenwood Publishing Group, 2006.

Web Sites

▶ **EnterUganda.com**
www.enteruganda.com
A general site with information on life in Uganda, both today and historically.

▶ **Isaac's House**
www.isaacshouse.org
To find out more about Isaac's House, an organization that helps Ugandan children who have been orphaned.

▶ **LEAD Uganda**
www.leaduganda.org
For information about a project that educates and cares for orphaned Ugandan children.

▶ NatureUganda
www.natureuganda.org
Detailed information on efforts to preserve Uganda's wildlife, including how to get involved.

▶ Tourism Uganda
www.visituganda.com
An excellent introduction to Uganda, its people, and its wildlife.

▶ The World Factbook: Uganda
www.cia.gov/library/publications/
the-world-factbook/geos/ug.html
A U.S. government country study with up-to-date statistics and background information.

Embassies

▶ **Embassy of the Republic of Uganda**
5911 16th Street, NW
Washington DC 20011
202-726-7100
www.ugandaembassy.com

▶ **Uganda High Commission, Ottawa, Canada**
231 Cobourg Street
Ottawa, Ontario
K1N 8J2
613-789-7797
www.ugandahighcommission.com

Index

Page numbers in *italics* indicate illustrations.

prayers, *94*, *97*, 98, *98*, 100
Protestantism, 47, 48, 96
Ramadan, 98
Roman Catholicism, 48, 59, 73,
    96, 97
Rubaga Catholic Cathedral, 73
traditional religions, 95, 99–101,
    99, *100*, 101, *101*
reptilian life, 36, 37, *37*
Ripon Falls, 19, 46
roadways, 39, 43, *53*, 81, 82, *82*, 107
Robinson, George, 46
Roman Catholicism, 48, 58, 73, 96, 97
Rotary Club, 93
Royal Ascot Goat Race, 122, *122*
Royal Speke Resort, 122
Rubaga Catholic Cathedral, 73
Rwanda, 13, 16, 26, 89
Rwenzori Mountains, 15, *15*, 38

S

Salisbury, Lord, 51, *51*
Semliki River, 22
service industries, 80–81, *80*
Sese Islands, *13*, 18, 22–23
Sheraton Hotel, 118, *118*
shillings (currency), 10, 83, *83*
Sipi Falls, *12*
soccer, 112–113, *113*
Speke, John Hanning, 20, 22,
    45–46, *46*
Spirit of Uganda dance group, *110*, 111
sports, 9, 81, *81*, 112–115, *112*, *113*,
    114, *115*

Sserulyo, Ignatius, 112
Sudan, 13, 16, 21, 22, 44, 63, 64, 65,
    82, 89
Suna (Buganda kabaka), 44
Supreme Court, 70–71
Swahili language, 89

T

Tanganyika, 49, 53, 57
Tanzania, 13, 18, 49, 62, 69
textiles, 51, 78–79, 105, *105*
tonal languages, 90
Toro Kingdom, 43, 49, 50, 69, *69*
tourism, 63, 75–76, *75*, 80
towns. *See also* cities; villages.
    Entebbe, 14, 19, 36, 61, *75*, 81,
        86, 93
    Gulu, 14, 82
    Internet service, 83
    Kilembe, *47*
    Kololo, 93
transportation, 9, 18, *18*, 19, 22, 39,
    52, 52, 54, 73, 81–82, *82*
tsetse flies, 32
TV stations, 83

U

ugali (porridge), 125
Uganda Christian University, 91
Uganda International Fashion
    Week, 78
Uganda Martyrs University, 91
Uganda National Congress (UNC), 58

Uganda National Liberation Army, 62
Uganda National Museum, 73, 107
Uganda Patriotic Movement, 63
Uganda People's Congress (UPC), 58
Uganda Railway, 51–52, *52*, 54
Uganda Wildlife Education Centre, 36
Universal Couple sculpture, 111
University of Mbale, 19, 91

V

Victoria Nile, 21, 32
Victoria, queen of Great Britain, 20
villages. *See also* cities, towns.
    agriculture, 123
    cooking, 124
    housing, *54*, 123–124, *123*
    international aid, 105
    water, 124, *124*
Virunga Mountains, 16

W

water hyacinth, 39, *39*
weevils, 39
weights and measures, 82
White Nile River, 19, 21, 22
white-water rafting, 81, *81*
wildlife. *See* animal life; insect life;
    marine life; plant life; reptilian
    life.
women, 70, 84, 87–88, *88*, 97, *97*,
    103, 105, 107, 119, 120, *120*
World War I, 53, *53*, 55
World War II, 55

Meet the Authors

JASON LAURÉ HAS PHOTOGRAPHED THE PEOPLE AND CUL-tures of 40 countries in Africa. From his first trip crossing the Sahara in 1970, he has learned about the continent from close contact with the people and the land. He finds the people of Uganda to be among the friendliest he has encountered. During his visits to Uganda, he has observed the country

emerging from its difficult history and becoming one of the most progressive nations in Africa. He tried out a boda-boda when he traveled to a white-water rafting area near the Nile River on a recent trip to Uganda.

Mr. Lauré was born in Chehalis, Washington, and attended Columbia University in New York City before working for the *New York Times*. He has written more than a dozen books in the Enchantment of the World series with his partner, Ettagale Blauer.

Ms. Blauer has traveled across Africa with Mr. Lauré, learning about cultures and gathering material for the many books they have written together. They have been through the gold and diamond mines of southern Africa and explored the jungles of central Africa. During Ms. Blauer's travels, she found the thirst for education in Uganda particularly inspiring. Wherever she went in Uganda, she says, people brought energy and enthusiasm to their work and their lives.

In addition to her writings for young adults, Ms. Blauer is the author of *African Elegance*, a book that explores the crafts and cultures of sub-Saharan Africa. Ms. Blauer was born in New York City and graduated from Hunter College.

Photo Credits